CASSELL STUDIES IN PASTORAL CARE AND PERSONAL
AND SOCIAL EDUCATION

TEACHERS, PUPILS AND BEHAVIOUR

A Managerial Approach

John McGuiness

CASSELL

Cassell
Villiers House, 41/47 Strand, London WC2N 5JE
387 Park Avenue South, New York, NY 10016–8810

First published 1993

British Library Cataloguing-in-Publication Data
A catalogue record for this book is available from the British
Library.

ISBN 0–304–32784–0 (hardback)
      0–304–32785–9 (paperback).

Typeset by Fakenham Photosetting Ltd, Fakenham, Norfolk
Printed and bound in Great Britain by
Biddles Ltd, Guildford and King's Lynn

Un pequeño homenaje a Sara Miranda, que sabe vivir.

Contents

Foreword

The publication in 1989 of the report of the committee of inquiry into school discipline, chaired by Lord Elton, was a significant event in the educational world of the 1980s. Here, for the first time, was an official report which addressed in a thoughtful and systematic way a serious and emotive issue in schooling. It was in many ways an enlightened document which recognized the important connections that exist between good management and the creation of an orderly and purposeful school environment in which pupils are likely to accept the authority of the teacher and the objectives of the school. In particular there was the recognition that whole-school problems call for whole-school responses.

Although 'the problem of discipline' is always with us, the Education Reform Act of 1988 has switched attention to other issues. Teachers and educationalists have rather less time to think constructively about the creation and maintenance of orderly social relations; they are too busy coming to terms with the requirements of the National Curriculum and the elaborate assessment procedures which accompany it, and in contemplating the promise and the problems of opting out of local authority control. The ideals of the Elton Report have not always been reflected in school development plans, where the emphasis is likely to be on curricular concerns linked to the need to make a good showing in the 'league tables' of school examination results.

Recent demands for more 'whole-class' teaching, greater grouping by ability (streaming by any other name) and a return to more regimented lessons imply a simplistic approach to matters of classroom control. Little thought is given to the relationship between classroom management, the organization and delivery of the curriculum, and reported increases in the incidence of bullying, pupil disaffection and soaring rates of pupil suspension.

We are delighted to include John McGuiness's book as the first in this new series because it adopts a more positive and penetrating perspective on these issues. Taking the ideals of the Elton Report as a starting point, the author builds a strong case for a rational and reflective approach to discipline which recognizes the distinction between exercising authority for purposes of control, and creating order in the educative process. The goal must be self-discipline built upon a realization of the rights of others: this is not only a prerequisite for education but also an aim of personal and social education itself.

Both teachers and pupils have rights, and it is integral to the ethos of the school as a caring community that mutual respect and tolerance should characterize classroom relations. These things do not come easily, however. This book will appeal to practising teachers precisely because it assesses realistically the scale of the challenge which pupil behaviour poses for them. In the long run, the only entirely satisfactory way of getting people to behave is to provide them with opportunities to develop to a point where they can take responsibility for themselves. The management of the learning experiences which schools provide must be guided by this principle.

Good management requires more than a few handy tips, and John McGuiness provides much more than this. We are invited to reflect upon our motives and our perceptions of the motives of others and to analyse critically the complex social contexts in which we operate. Finally, we are provided with a variety of staff development activities and questions for discussion which link theory to practice, strategy to principle. The result is a book which is both useful and challenging, and which relocates a perennial concern in the context of the school's responsibility to care for its members and actively to promote their personal and social development.

Peter Lang
Ron Best

Acknowledgements

I would like to express my thanks to the Research Committee of the School of Education at Durham University for a grant which helped to make it possible for me to complete this book. I am also most grateful to my colleagues Peter Cook, Mike Fleming and Jack Gilliland, who were willing to cover my responsibilities in the Department during my absence.

John McGuiness

Note

to the reader

In your shoes, I find it difficult not to skip introductions to books – no doubt a character failing on my part. Empathy with those who have a similar character weakness leads me to be brief here.

I was, as a schoolteacher, very warmed by Paul Francis's encouraging book, *Beyond Control* (1975). Now, as a university teacher, I am made cautious by his wise observation that our ideas about responding to the challenging pupil become more confident and assertive the further away we are from the classroom. I have never felt that confidence or assertiveness on such matters, and any reader who has bought this text looking for such qualities should ask for a refund now! I am convinced that, such is the subtlety of the challenge, our response must be of equal or greater subtlety – experimental in the real sense of that word, that is, not locked into prejudices about procedures or preconceptions about outcomes. To be, unapologetically, managerial.

John McGuiness
Villasinta, León, 1992

CHAPTER 1

Take aim

Some key introductory thoughts

A friend in industrial management once surprised me by saying, 'I don't have much problem in formulating *answers* to questions. My biggest difficulty is making sure that I'm answering the *right questions*.' I have a horrible suspicion that I have spent too much time in classrooms answering the wrong questions. My justification for adding to the acres of print dedicated to pupil behaviour is that this book will stick to a problem-solving approach, in which the reader has the initiative. The case material will be stimulus material, not recipe material. It will ask for an honest, professional sharing of perceptions, and since answers are always school- or teacher-specific, it will not be able to provide any general answers. It will try to identify some of the right questions. There has always been a tendency to seek some panacea that would leave teachers and classrooms free from disruption – behaviour modification, esteem enhancement, withdrawal units, more effective curricular matching, reality therapy, confluent education: the list is endless, and all of the elements on it are useful. The error is to expect one strategy to respond to the complex demands of managing a classroom.

John Sayer (1988) skilfully uses an analysis of management, which he attributes to De Bono, to look at the demands made of teachers. Four activities are seen as symbolizing the different modes of management required from us: train driving (with its predictability, reliance on everyone following the rules, clarity of task); medicine (with the attendant calls on emergency response, health promotion and ability to return from crisis to status quo); farming (the attempt to achieve maximum yield from variable land, seed, equipment, weather); and rod fishing (the speculative cast of the line, relying on a judicious interplay of experience, instinct, intuition and hunch). Managing classrooms involves all four types of activity, and thus *must* transcend any attempt to simplify it into a unidimensional response. The challenge to each teacher individually, and each school corporately, is to develop a 'creative synthesis' of all of the strategies available. That involves maximizing the knowledge base, clarifying the values which underpin decision-making, enhancing the widest possible repertoire of relationship and communication skills. It is a dynamic, constantly changing process, which is reviewed, then started afresh, almost minute by minute in the classroom. Fundamentally, effective classroom management is about the skill of decision-making.

A writer needs to avoid both the seductive attraction of recipe provision and what, to the reader, can seem an infuriating abdication of responsibility for taking a clear, personal position on the issue. Let me try to walk that line. I have learned from and used packs, but find them too simple for a general application to classroom challenge. I have gradually come to realize (thanks in no small measure to the sensitive questions posed to the profession in the Elton Report, 1989), that pupil behaviour is motivated by such a wide range of influences – and teacher responses to that pupil behaviour drawn, often implicitly, from such a complex background of cognitive, developmental, social and intrapersonal psychology – that the professional challenge is to match the teacher's available resources to the pursuit of clearly defined objectives, in a climate of which I am as fully as possible aware. From a managerial standpoint, the demand on us as teachers is to clarify our educational objectives, to scrutinize all the resources at our disposal for the pursuit of those objectives, and to understand in detail the environmental influences within which we work. That is the basis of our pupil behaviour management strategies.

This book tackles the key elements outlined above by presenting a summary of relevant knowledge bases, drawn largely from the social sciences, and by offering a series of activities, case material and exercises that invite a reflective application of some of the pertinent theory to the classrooms in which we work. Its flexible form permits its use by a wide range of people involved in education. Many of the exercises were piloted on initial teacher education courses, with members of the business community and with adults other than teachers who are involved on governing bodies and PTAs.

At the heart of the exercises is a commitment to the concept of collective wisdom, of sharing skills (and anxieties) in a way that encourages all the members of a working group to try out new ways of responding to the challenge of pupil behaviour. The final chapter draws together some of the exercises into a suggested 12-hour module for use in initial teacher training, INSET or governor training. However, each chapter is a self-contained exploration of a key element in managing, and the exercises which conclude each chapter can be used separately from the others.

It seems important, in this opening chapter, to share with the reader some of my preoccupations, starting points and vision of how we might develop classroom management skills. It is a scene-setter, a declaration of intent, a clarifier of concepts. Chapter 2 takes us straight into case material, not merely to stretch our problem-solving capacity, but to illustrate the enormous complexity of the behaviours children bring to the classroom. In Chapter 3 a fundamental aspect of all management is presented – managers as change-agents: they, we in the classroom, are charged with the task of getting people to change, academically, socially, emotionally, behaviourally. And we intend that change to be positive. How do human beings react to the invitation to change and what can I, as a manager, do to facilitate the demanding changes I ask of my pupils? The central role played by values in decision-making is analysed in Chapter 4. The values that drove the 1944 Education Act are different from the ones that power the 1988 Education Reform Act – and so the decisions made are very different. To understand decisions we need to go beyond logic to values, and this applies as much to our personal decisions in the classroom as to the great decisions of state. Gelatt (1962) observed how frequently this key element in decision-making has remained unscrutinized, thus rendering a precise evaluation of those decisions virtually impossible. The business world has taken this on board. It merits our attention, too, as managers in classrooms. Our decisions are driven by our values. But we are not robotic decision-makers; we use logic and are influenced by values – and we feel. Chapter 5 responds to the increasing body of research data that indicate the impossibility of dichotomizing the professional persona from the real person. We may try to repress our feelings during our professional activity, yet however controlled we may appear to be, those feelings have their influence on us. The need for a feeling of self-worth is a central influence on the behaviour of all of us in classrooms. Defence of damaged self-esteem by both teachers and pupils is probably the key factor in the initiation and development of disruptive incidents.

Up to this point the book concentrates on the vast majority of pupils who are not fundamentally damaged; the pupils for whom sensitive pedagogy and challenge with support is the essential input. Yet all of us have come across the small percentage of pupils who come to us damaged or who are so challenged by the experience of school that they resist it in extremely disruptive ways. Chapter 6 examines critical incidents, trying not to offer a list-based response programme but to develop in the teacher an awareness of key interpersonal and group skills that can defuse difficult situations. Chapter 7 looks at wider organizational strategies, putting school ethos, the curriculum, case conferences, contracting with pupils, behaviour modification and counselling on our broader response agenda. Individual teachers work within their own school's climate, and to do so most effectively requires a high degree of match between the two. As was mentioned above, the final chapter suggests a training module which draws on the material to be found at the end of each chapter. Extra resources are added in the Appendix.

Here, then, are my cards on the table. The central demands made of teachers by the National Curriculum – to offer a broad and balanced diet which promotes the spiritual, moral, cultural, mental and physical development of pupils and prepares them for adult life – are not accompanied by any legal requirements on methodology. We are given a complex task, and, like any other managers, we should be left to get on with it. This text will raise issues about the 'how', with special reference to pupil behaviour. If pupils will not work with us, we cannot help them to learn – horses to water, and all that. An initial skill for us is to create the most facilitative learning environment possible for the majority of pupils who are basically cooperative. But we need to develop, too, the ability to respond to the time-consuming but numerically small number of extremely taxing young people who can drain us of energy. The book addresses three core issues: what kind of a person do I need to be to encourage pupils to take the risks involved in learning? What do I need to be able to do? And what ought I to know?

There is a sense in which the question of the incidence of disruptive behaviour and whether or not this has increased in recent years is a red herring. It may be useful for union representatives negotiating pay settlements and governments looking at performance indicators, but for the teacher facing challenging pupil behaviour such large contextual considerations offer small comfort. The central challenge for such a teacher is to devise strategies that will pre-empt such behaviour, or increase the ability to respond to it in a way that is not damagingly stressful to the teacher, harmful to the learning of other pupils in the class or destructive, in some way, of the dignity of the misbehaving pupil. Despite the above, those who wish to check the extent to which 'things have got worse' will find the research (typically?) ambiguous. Tattum (1982), Smith (1989), Graham (1972) and the Elton Report (DES, 1989) properly decline to make comparisons over time, given that the evidence is simply not available.

It is clear that most teachers at some time face stressful challenges to their authority. Whether the situation is more difficult now than previously is not the concern of this text. It is my intention to scrutinize the current scene, with special reference to the Elton Report (1989), and to work on strategies that will reduce teacher stress, permit productive classroom work to continue and allow the teacher to respond to the negative pupil in a way that, despite the pupil's initial unattractiveness, recognizes the human dignity that lies behind the often gross exterior. It is a tall order, and one I accept with some trepidation, only because of the many professional development courses I have shared with colleagues on this topic. The ideas here have been elaborated alongside literally hundreds of teachers since 1985, and spring from both classroom-based and university-based work.

Some teachers survive in difficult classrooms by adopting strategies that are costly in terms of their physical and mental health. Many colleagues with whom I work in management consultancy are astounded at the absence of support from a personnel department for the most valuable resource for children's learning – the teacher. Given evidence like that accumulated by the International Labour Organisation (1981), Kyriacou (1986) and Dunham (1984) that teacher stress is not only personally damaging but also educationally counterproductive, then the strong recommendations of Elton are timely, and must not be shelved.

I hope you will find this book practical, that it can help change the way in which you work to a mode which feels more comfortable, satisfying and educationally effective. Most pupils are not monsters, and part of the challenge to teacher skill is to work with the normally well behaved, but occasionally taxing, pupil. It would, nevertheless, be less than professional for us not to examine very carefully the outrageous behaviour of the few, and to develop ways of responding to that, too.

Discussion with school-based colleagues at all stages of their professional life suggests that pupil aggression (Elton's evidence indicates that this is rarely physical: 1989: 11,3) saps energy and confidence, even among experienced teachers. It is hard to admit to disciplinary difficulties, and we are socialized early in our professional life into a resilient silence. Several LEAs are now hard at work to make problem disclosures less difficult, yet during the early days of the Durham project with young teachers and their difficult pupils, we were constantly quizzed about the use to which honest disclosures might be put – in decisions about probation, promotion and references for new jobs (McGuiness and Craggs, 1986). Senior managers must take on board the idea that underperformance in the area of classroom management can create a collusive silence between the teacher-victim and the busy senior manager. Both have at least a superficial interest in the non-disclosure of difficulty.

The reality, of course, is that aside from the human damage that is being done, the medium- and long-term result of such a failure to confront the problem at the earliest possible moment is considerable for both the school and individual pupils. This presents all senior management in education with the task of creating a professional, supportive forum for the fullest analysis at all levels of reasons for pupil misbehaviour. We need, for example, to recognize that different children, classes and schools present a challenge of enormous variation – which needs to be *managed*. The 'in-at-the-deep-end' style of management is the teaching equivalent of leaving a new recruit to run a small-scale factory or office. As a senior manager I need to ask how I can best use my available resources to face current tasks. Most heads do this, but it is still the case that probationers and students (licensed and articled teachers, too, I imagine) are given very difficult classes to teach without appropriate support. There are clear resource implications here, and managers cannot do the job without them. The Elton Report (1989) is unequivocal in its support for teachers on this point: 'levels of expenditure on teachers, schools and support services vary considerably from LEA to LEA ... figures show a range of expenditure estimates for secondary schools from about £1500 to £2500 per pupil'. If Elton is to be taken seriously, then adequate resourcing is a major theme. One recommendation (R12) suggests that 'Secretaries of State and LEAs should give due weight to the serious implications of any actual or predicted teacher shortages ... when considering future pay levels and conditions of service for the profession.'

All of our creativity with regard to practice can be vitiated if we are not properly resourced. That is one of a number of factors which have a strong influence on pupil behaviour, and over which we have minimal control. It is important to establish the parameters of the school's responsibility if we are not to become some kind of media scapegoat for everything from poll-tax riots to child abuse.

As part of the recent government initiative to draw together the worlds of business and education (Enterprise Awareness in Teacher Education), I recently worked with businessmen on some case material of incidents of disruption. They were astonished at the complexity of classroom decision-making and the room for error. I have certainly gained from my contacts with the world of business – business people's commitment to excellence, willingness to monitor and evaluate, constant openness to change and new ideas and, significantly, their humility in facing case material on pupil misbehaviour. It was a salutary reminder to me of the high level of professional skill required of teachers. There is no more taxing managerial challenge than that of responding, *as a teacher*, to pupil misbehaviour. I emphasize 'as a teacher' to distinguish the educator's response from that of the policeman. We are expected to do more than simply maintain order – and therein lies the difficulty of our task.

CHAPTER 2

Data overload

The origins of misbehaviour

The previous chapter gave some indication of how response to pupils' misbehaviour needs to be as complex as the causes of that misbehaviour. Using Sayer's (1988) modes of managerial activity, outlined in the first chapter, we can see that as train-drivers, doctors, farmers and people who fish, our managerial tasks are many and interactive. This chapter will try to put some flesh on to the nature of that complexity and apply some of the emergent ideas to a case study.

Schools do not exist in a vacuum, nor do teachers work in a climate unaffected by the larger, different worlds within which we and our pupils live. We can see in Figure 2.1 some of the factors which complicate the challenge to our professional skill.

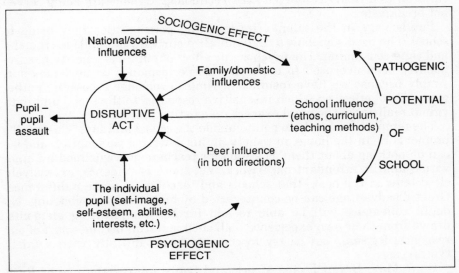

Figure 2.1 Interacting factors influencing pupil behaviour: sociogenic, psychogenic and potentially pathogenic or child-damaging effect of school response.

The fact that the case material presented at the end of this chapter occurred shortly after the long miners' strike and the later teachers' industrial action (during 1983 and 1984) is an immediate reminder that part of the crystallization of values for both pupils and ourselves is the national social scene. Attitudes to power, influence, possessions, equity, gentleness, justice, gender, race and so on pervade our lives via television, radio, popular music, newspapers and magazines. Does strike action by parents or teachers influence pupil perspectives on pursuing objectives? What, if anything, do pupils bring into the classroom from their experience of factory or pit closures, redundancy or the bankruptcy of a family firm? Even if we cannot measure it, there is sufficient research evidence on the impact of such events on adults (Jahoda, 1979, 1981) to establish a strong *prima facie* case that similar effects will be found in children. We do not create the problems, but we operate with the consequences.

The individual child's family, too, can seep negatively (and, of course, positively) into the classroom. I recently came across a primary school child at 11 a.m. who had last eaten at school lunch the previous day. We do not need to have expertise in the effects of low blood sugar levels to suppose some effect of that child's experience on her learning and response to teachers. And what of homes with no books, no tradition of valuing education, or with sexist or racist attitudes? All complicate our attempts to make an educational response to our pupils. These so-called sociogenic effects are not within our power to change, but we do need to recognize that they are part of our problem-solving challenge. I find it ironic that the primary school child mentioned above lives in a deprived inner-city area in the north of England, and that a few miles away children in a richly resourced City Technology College are being served hot breakfasts.

Pupils vary in the talents, interest and personalities they bring to school. The need somehow to individualize our view of pupils is crucial -- and time-consuming. The psychogenic effect of pupil personality has frequently been overused to explain underperformance or misbehaviour, simply because we have insufficient time to consider a possible pathogenic school effect, in which insensitive responses to the social and individual realities of the pupil exacerbate existing problems.

The temptation simply to point outside the school and say, 'This pupil's problems lie in the home, in society, in his defective personality, and we can do nothing about them' is strong for teachers overwhelmed by innovation and its attendant paperwork. Yet there is evidence, extensively cited later in the book, that schools and teachers *do* make a difference. Great disadvantage can be counteracted by highly skilled schooling. No doubt colleagues will be able to add further complicating elements, drawn from their own experience – all such material becomes part of our response decision. Let us try to come to terms initially with a fairly typical case.

On 7 May, Bryan Evans struck and badly injured the eye of Ruth Taylor at 4.15 p.m., on the way home from school. Both are in the fourth year of Collpit Comprehensive School. There it is in its simplicity – and complexity. Teacher readers will already be formulating lines of investigation, possible questions, strategies for action. The non-teacher, too, may feel intellectually challenged by the incident – as were my business colleagues who tackled the problem.

An initial reaction of one business colleague was, 'Thank God it was after school. It's not our concern.' We had a long discussion about the extent of our responsibility and decided that, on balance, we had to take some action. My view is that 99 per cent of teachers would follow up such an occurrence. Here are the details assembled from the subsequent investigation. It is not a test to see if we can come up with the right answer – there isn't one; it is simply an example to non-teacher readers (governors, PTAs, LEA administrators) of the detail required to respond to one school incident. It is also useful to the classroom practitioner as a reminder of how frequently we all make our decisions without a full review of the facts.

Name:	Bryan Evans
Age:	14 years 3 months
Father:	Unemployed fitter
Mother:	Part-time machinist in a local clothing factory
Parents:	39 years and 36 years respectively
Siblings:	M – Thomas 18 Barry 16 Alan 8
	F – Patricia 15 Barbara 12 Ann 10

Bryan has been a challenging pupil since his arrival in the school almost four years ago. Academically, he has barely developed the skills he brought from primary school. He has the reading age of an eight-year-old and he never voluntarily reads anything. His attitude in class suggests total boredom and, until recently, silent non-cooperation.

In the last two months Bryan has begun to be insolent to teachers and aggressive to peers. We suspect, too, that he vandalized the art room during the lunch break, but have only circumstantial evidence of this. He vehemently denies the vandalism. In the past two weeks the following incidents have occurred:

3 May: split lip of second-year boy who was 'was getting on my wick' during the lunch break.

5 May: swore at the art teacher who had told him to tidy up some paint he had spilt. As usual there was a dispute about whether he was the guilty party.

7 May (at 4.15, on the way home from school): badly injured the eye of a fourth-year girl, not in his class, who he claimed had called him a 'puff'.

10 May: having left the deputy head's office following an interview about the Friday evening incident, he was immediately ejected from his English class, where his return was described by the teacher as 'disruptive, inappropriate and rude'.

14 May: probationary teacher withdrew from his class, reporting immediately to the deputy head that Bryan had destroyed his control over the group.

Immediate reactions run the gamut shown in Figure 2.1. Is Bryan bringing into school lessons about violence and respect for persons that he is learning from videos, from TV news reports about football violence, from mythologies about the miners' or the teachers' strike? If so, school influence over such sociogenic effects will be limited. Limited too, though not non-existent, is the school's countervailing effect on strong family values. The curriculum may be seen by his teachers to be inflexibly inappropriate, though it seems likely that greater recognition will soon be given to teacher decision-making in the implementation of the National Curriculum. So many influences over which teacher control is greatly constrained ... It is important for us not to feel responsible for these influences, though, as Watts (1983) put it in a different context, they may not be educational problems, but they are problems for educationalists. We need to face up to them, recognizing that although they are not of our making, they do come within the area of our responsibility. It is reassuring to find such consistency in research that indicates that schools *do* make a difference. Rutter and his colleagues (1979), Reynolds and Sullivan (1987) and Mortimore *et al.* (1988) find that, while we can identify some causative elements in the social and family backgrounds of pupils, a significant ameliorating effect, with particular reference to pupil behaviour, is achieved by certain kinds of schools and teaching styles.

But let us return to Bryan. Beyond the influences outside of the school, we need to look carefully, in collaboration with our colleagues in the Schools Psychological Service, at possible psychogenic causes. One of the businessmen who looked at this case study commented, 'This lad seems a bit of a nutter. Should teachers be facing this kind of rubbish?' I imagine the wry smiles of teacher readers who will have asked themselves the same question on more than one occasion. The reality seems to be that it is fortunately rare for us to have to face a mentally ill pupil, but mental illness, like physical illness, is not a yes–no concept. The severely disturbed child is quickly identified, referred to colleagues in other institutions and taught there. Nevertheless, the question asked by the businessman was serious. And so must be our answer.

Teachers are asked to face seriously damaged children who, because their sense of personal worth is negligible (and consequently their ability to see worth in other people), are mentally ill. They are few in number, but Jones's (1975) study, finding that only 0.9 per cent of pupils identified by school as maladjusted are referred to child guidance units, can be seen in the light of later studies by ILEA (1986, 1988), which indicate that secondary schools exclude about ten times as many pupils as primary schools. Mortimore *et al.* (1988), collecting data at about the same time, found that in a study of fifty junior schools, teachers rated about 5 per cent of the pupils aggressive. There can be no doubt that the profession is being called upon to deal with very challenging pupils. An excellent survey of current research into this area has been compiled by Smith (1989).

So, is Bryan a 'nutter'? In the sense that Cantor (1984) defines 'dementia' (loss of ability to be rational), almost certainly not, but in the sense that he is damaged, yes. As far back as 1968 the Summerfield

Report recognized the reality of this teaching task: 'The British Psychological Society does not hold that no one but a psychologist should advise on signs of stress, and the Society would welcome a dissemination of appropriate psychological knowledge among teachers.' Part of our responsibility is to respond in a psychologically apt way to this pupil, making a referral when this is judged appropriate.

A more detailed database was accumulated following the assault on the fourth-year girl:

The social worker reported that the home was materially comfortable (good furniture, colour TV and video, hi-fi) but rather untidy. Dirty clothes on the floor, sink full of dirty dishes, beds unmade.

Bryan's form tutor reported that conversations with him indicated that there was no fixed bedtime for any of the children, and that the parents were frequently out when the children went to bed. He also commented on the intense loyalty to parents shown by Bryan. During a tutorial exercise, Bryan had said that his greatest fear in life was, 'if me Mam died'. There is warmth in the family and a kind of rough justice reigns. Nevertheless, discipline is based on quite brutal physical punishment, which is accepted on both sides as normal. When asked by the deputy head what would happen if the school reported the assault to his father, Bryan had replied, 'He'll kill me.'

Bryan is popular with male peers (he is a good athlete), but his capacity for leadership can be used disruptively. It is quite clear that his disruption is selective: i.e. it occurs with specific teachers or subjects. This merits careful professional attention. Figure 2.1 suggests that in addition to sociogenic and psychogenic causes there can also exist a number of pathogenic effects in the school. (An extensive literature raises the challenging concept of the child-damaging or pathogenic school: Power et al., 1967; Reynolds, 1976; Rutter et al., 1979; Schostak, 1982; Steed et al., 1983; McGuiness and Craggs, 1986.)

A final trawl of available data from Bryan's teachers revealed the following discrepant views of the issue:

Art. This boy should be in care. He is a danger to himself and to others. [While this reaction is absolutely understandable, it does emphasize the sociogenic and psychogenic, to the exclusion of a possibly inadequate school response to the needs of Bryan. The professional reality is that Bryan will probably remain in the school, so the luxury of pushing responsibility out of school in the direction of society, family or the pupil's personality is not a possibility. An analysis of the effect of the school's intervention, with its potential for either pathogenic or facilitative results, is needed. Again, see Figure 2.1.]

English. Bryan's reading is abysmal. He shows no interest and tries actively to destroy the interest of other pupils. [Where the previous comment tended to be judgemental, this one does make a number of statements about the pupil's work and behaviour. The implicit professional challenge is to respond to the question, How can we help him improve his reading and his social skills?]

Geography. Bryan is a lively lad – a poor reader, but excellent in projects or activities involving manual skills. No scholar. [It is clear that the picture is not one of unmitigated gloom. A case conference can identify areas or individuals with potential for positive effect. It should not be regarded as a competitive issue that different teachers are successful with specific pupils. From a managerial point of view it is crucial to develop in staff a collaborative approach to problems of pupil behaviour. Given Elton's comments on resources (1989: R12), it is also pertinent to comment that a differential salary scale based on shortage subjects could have devastating effects on responses to misbehaviour. The able mathematician who needs support in disciplinary and pastoral matters may, indefensibly, be left to stew in his own juice.]

History. This boy is the bane of my life. He is a constant disruptive influence. [A *cri de coeur*, in which there is no suggestion of positive possibilities. Is there no project work in history? If there is, what can I learn from my geography colleague's limited success with Bryan? Here a sharing in a case conference can enhance the professional development of all concerned. It will not simply happen, it needs to be worked for. A successful use of the case conference depends centrally on senior management's ability to create a supportive, professional ambience.]

Maths. No interest shown. The boy is either bored or disruptive, never industrious. [The teacher appears to be identifying the consequences of rigid curricular requirements. Of course Bryan needs maths, but it may be that an inflexible approach based on standard assessment tasks is not what is needed. A creative use of the special educational needs provisions of the 1988 Education Reform Act may be helpful.]

PE. Bryan is a willing, able boy. He willingly spends hours helping to mark pitches, set up nets and care for equipment. [Clearly, as with the geographer, the PE teacher has a productive relationship with the pupil. This ought not to be devalued, but used. Occasionally, teachers who are able to establish successful relationships with difficult pupils are regarded with scant respect by colleagues. This is another area of responsibility for the headteacher, who must see this ability as a positive resource and persuade all colleagues to the same view. It may be that some maths can be pursued in PE – again the case conference needs to be creatively managed.]

RE. Despite occasional disruption, this boy has a thoughtful side. He talks thoughtfully about his family and has an ability and willingness to discuss moral issues. [The impact of socio-emotional factors on pupils' performance, academically or behaviourally, cannot be overemphasized. The case conference provides a much wider and more useful range of possible responses to Bryan's educational needs than the single interview with a member of staff.]

Science. Bryan will do experimental and practical work with zeal. He writes badly, but speaks perceptively about experiments. Lately, he has acted dangerously in the lab, but responded positively when I spoke quietly to him. [Here is a teacher claiming that this 'nutter' responds positively to a quiet reprimand – as a colleague intent on broadening my skills, I want to learn how he does it, and the case conference is an ideal place to do so.]

For the moment, I want simply to leave Bryan there, with no answers but with a mass of questions. Good managers seek useful, operable data by asking astute questions. Solutions to problems are found by learning to ask the right questions. As an initial exercise (if it feels comfortable) try the following task:

Either:
Invite each group member to adopt the character of one of the people in the case study. Ask the group leader to chair a conversation between the participants, with the simple purpose of seeing the problem from as many points of view as possible.

Or:
If role play feels a bit too risky, simply discuss reactions to the case material as openly as possible. It is important to accept at the outset that there cannot be a right answer, and to encourage everyone to give as honestly as possible his or her ideas of where to go next.

I hope to have set a scene and a theme. The scene must, for us, be the school in general and the classroom in particular. The theme is creative response, respect for our skills and values as a profession, and a round rejection of recipes and package approaches to professional challenge. It may well be that after the exploration suggested above, the significance of Sayer's 'managerial modes' becomes clearer. Bryan requires us to 'manage' him in the engine-driver mode, with its expectations of operating within common values (about violence and aggression), with a degree of predictability (not unilaterally changing the rules halfway between King's Cross and Newcastle – or history and geography), and with some agreement and commitment to timetables and schedules. We can say, 'Right! Either conform or crash!' (Exclusion?) The doctor mode of management *expects* all that crisis and unpredictability, and Bryan certainly makes calls on our ability to steer back from crisis to status quo and health. And we have to do it at the same time as driving the train! Nor is that all, since the managerial 'farmer' in us has to drive, cure and *produce* from this unpredictable seed, in the vagaries of a domestic and social climate over which we have minimal control. Finally, the fisherman (or woman) in us needs intuition beyond the obvious, to fish in the murky waters of Bryan Evans in the hope that my hunch will let me catch some real potential in Bryan and help it germinate.

I hope that at the very outset I acknowledge the complexity of the skills required of the teacher-manager, and the formidable challenge latent in any apparently simple incident of pupil misbehaviour.

CHAPTER 3

Managing nicely

On being a professional

The case of Bryan Evans illustrates clearly the contentions of the DES (1987) booklet *Good Behaviour and Discipline in Schools*, that 'The most important of these external influences is that of the parents and the home', that 'society at large does not consistently exemplify high standards of behaviour' and that 'society has high expectations of its schools'. The Elton Report, strangely commissioned just a year after the publication of the detailed DES report, and itself published in 1989, arrived at similar broad conclusions, and re-emphasized the interlocking complex of factors that teachers need to weigh in making decisions about pupil behaviour: 'the behaviour of pupils in a school is influenced by almost every aspect of the way in which it is run and how it relates to the community' (DES, 1989, Foreword, 5). It is part of the argument of this book that while discrete elements of response to pupil challenge can and should be identified, practised and implemented, we do ourselves a disservice if we give the impression that such response can be straightforward.

I recently spoke to a thirteen-year-old Spaniard who was spending a term in a local comprehensive school to improve his language skills. He had been impressed by the many individual kindnesses he had received from both fellow pupils and teachers, on a personal and academic level, but he expressed surprise at the overall strictness of the atmosphere in comparison with his school in Spain. The uniform rules (especially the tie, something he had never worn) he found puzzling; and coming from a country where most girls get their first earrings at their christening, he was amazed at the jewellery regulations. He made a general comment about the noise level of teacher voices: 'Why do they shout so loud?', he asked. It was interesting to receive an 'extraterrestrial' view of a school I knew well and respected. Particularly amusing and informative was his view of the response when the head entered the room. 'We all have to *stop* work,' he said (my italics). I am quite sure that the purpose of the school practice here was based on a desire to develop courtesy and respect. What my young friend had learned was that the arrival of the head meant a cessation of work. I asked him about his school. 'Well, what would you do in Spain, when the head comes in?' 'Oh, we'd continue working and someone close to him might say, "hola Jorge".' I studied his face to see whether the 'Hi George' was being offered as an example of impertinence. Not a sign of it. It was meant as nothing more than a friendly greeting from one person to another.

Of course, cross-cultural comparisons are difficult, and I have no wish to get into sterile debates about uniforms, jewellery and the use of first or second names. What I do want to do is suggest that our answers to these issues are not inevitable or infallible. We *choose* our answers, and as professionals we need to scrutinize them. One of Elton's helpful insights is to construe the problem of disruptive behaviour as a challenge to our *management* skills. A consequence of this is to move smartly away from a rigid application of sets of behavioural norms towards a problem-solving posture, which responds creatively to challenges as they occur within the broad, clearly declared, consensual objectives of the school. I will argue that the issue is not centrally one of *control* – in the final analysis, we can always do that. Control is a policing activity. The real challenge, as Elton insists, is the far more complex one of creating the kinds of environments within which all of our pupils have a chance to make the most of their talent. That is not to police; that is to teach.

If the issues to be examined here are primarily issues of management, they must involve the teacher in *reflective* practice. No professional manager would accept the idea of operating according to some manual which removed his responsibility and de-professionalized his activity. Managing involves defining the problem or challenge to be responded to, data collection and analysis, clarity of objectives and the ability to implement them. It requires a sense of responsibility, room to manoeuvre, a large repertoire of possible responses – in a word, creativity. How frustrating it is, then, to find that much of the initial and in-service professional development work for teachers is the static 'recipe' type. While a beginning cook may feel reassured by the comforting predictability of the recipe book, the classy chef rapidly moves beyond that to something more personal and creative. There is a real danger that limited resources, especially time, may tempt us to reach for the recipe book. They have their uses, but they can turn us into very unimaginative operators.

Despite their attempts to fend us off and persuade us otherwise, our pupils are far more complex than bags of flour, lumps of lard and sacks of potatoes. They deserve – indeed, if they are to prosper they need – more than a recipe response. Reference to a manual fails to acknowledge the range of complex elements identified in DES (1987) and the Elton Report (DES, 1989). The nature of a professional manager's job makes it unacceptable for him or her to say, 'The manual doesn't work', or 'it doesn't cover this eventuality'. I can imagine a managing director's tart reply to such a comment. 'If we had wanted someone to operate according to a manual we wouldn't have employed a manager.' This may come across as harsh, but it is an indicator of total respect for the professional autonomy of teachers. We can no more learn to manage a classroom by reading books than we can improve our golf, drive our cars, or even make love. What books can do is help us to formulate questions, define problems clearly, replace hunch and implicit theory with well-established research as a basis for action, and help us to get into contact with the values and attitudes through which all our professional practice is filtered.

Let us get straight into some questions. Why do pupils misbehave? Do I misbehave? Are there certain situations, encounters, people that provoke a reactive hostility? What are they for me? For my pupils? Are some of these questions tougher than others – honestly? What kinds of component go into answering a question? Do I know enough? Am I open enough? Do I have the skills needed? Knowledge, values and skills – a safe, three-legged stool upon which sits the secure teacher. And three basic questions: What do I need to know, to be able to do, and 'who' do I need to be?

The most powerful way to examine the behaviour of our pupils is to look with great care at our own behaviour. There is not some great divide between the reactions of children, young people and adults to the situations and events they are asked to face. The developmental psychologists do offer us indicators of appropriate, age-related behaviour (Piaget and Inhelder, 1969; Blocher, 1974; Erikson, 1965) but all of them contain to varying degrees an important concept elaborated by Heisler (1961). She argues that development is the result of an interplay between the person and the environment, and, crucially, that to engage positively with the environment the person needs a secure base, a strong feeling of safety. She describes this phenomenon in terms of two organismic tendencies: a productive tension between stability and 'differentiation'. All of us, no matter what our age, face challenge, take risks, reach out to new ideas in a more effective way when we do so in an environment which lets us feel safe.

If this idea has currency it not only has implications for our pupils and the presence or absence of safety in the classroom environment, but also has some potentially powerful implications for the adult in a learning environment. In my own professional development I am subject to the same need for a liberating feeling of being safe as the pupil in my class. Further, it may be that by studying my own experience as a learner I will gain insight into the processes that lead my pupils into industrious cooperation or disruptive behaviour. A constant feature of our lives today is rapid change – internationally, nationally, socially, domestically and professionally. We are asked to interact with an environment that frequently feels far from safe. I ask myself how I reacted to ROSLA, CSE, GCSE, CPVE, TVEI, SATs, LFM, LMS and that whole army of acronyms redolent of underprepared changes to well-established practice. I confess to anger, truculence, resistance, a temptation to opt out and hope it would go away – just like a pupil who, rightly or wrongly, feels overstretched and undersupported.

It is normal for all of us, pupil and teacher alike, to react in this cautious, defensive way to novelty, and it is the task of the effective manager to devise strategies and create climates in which we rise to the challenge with courage. By considering the development of our teacher response to the recommendations of the Elton Report in parallel to pupil responses to our teaching we can gain important insights into some of the fundamental elements of effective management.

During a recent professional development day, I was introduced by the headteacher as the person who would lead the workshop on pastoral care. After the usual courtesies the head concluded by handing over the proceedings to me. As I stood up, I noticed immediately that two of the staff, rather ostentatiously, took out newspapers and began to read them! Although at first glance it seemed like a crude snub, in reality it was nothing more than two colleagues demonstrating, in the face of curricular novelty, the 'anger, truculence, resistance and opting out' to which I confessed two paragraphs earlier. That is not to defend it – but it does begin to explain how a pair of fellow-professionals could behave towards a stranger in a way which was, at best, discourteous and, perhaps more importantly, hurtful. Equally, it provides a nice parallel with what our pupils sometimes do to us. Having the boot on the other foot, with the new perspective that gives, is a salutary learning experience. I needed to devise a means of inviting the group to explore the occurrence, but in a way that left us all feeling more comfortable with each other, not more at risk.

I was quite used to responding with varied success to disruptive pupils – disruptive colleagues was a new experience. I felt all the *déjà vu* that came from my days as a young teacher – do I turn a blind eye? try to act the heavy? act as the reasonable, injured third party? try to use the incident in some way?

'I wonder if I can begin with a brief exercise,' I tried tentatively. Rustle of newspapers, but no lowering. 'We're about to spend six hours working together. I'd like you to imagine as many ways as possible of wasting the day, fouling it up. Just call out an idea, however outrageous it may seem. Be as unprofessional as you can think.' I had begun to realize that the majority of the staff had not noticed their reluctant colleagues and their newspapers. Very quickly we filled a flip-chart with the most impressive list of ways to waste a day. Eventually it came. One colleague called out, 'We could just ignore you and read our newspapers.' There was some laughter as the offending documents were folded and tucked away. I had hoped to get this opportunity to raise the reaction of the two members of staff, in a non-confrontational way, on to the public agenda. It seemed that what they were doing (and what many of us, I suspect, have often felt like doing at in-service sessions) contained an incredibly rich vein for learning about the relationship between learning and the feeling of being safe in the learning environment.

I apologized to the two colleagues, who had begun to smile too, for putting them under the spotlight, and explained that it was not simply the whim of a deranged Geordie. What I wanted to do, with their permission, was to use the incident to elucidate some key principles relating generically to management and more specifically both to our own professional development and to the learning of our pupils. The colleagues concerned agreed in a highly professional way to explore in detail their semi-automatic protest against what they expected me to do. 'Well,' said one, 'I'm a mathematician. I'm not trained or interested in being trained in pseudo-social-work.' Let us set on one side the arguments in favour of whole-school approaches to pastoral care, which was the topic of the workshop, and concentrate on the process of resistance to a new experience. His colleague, a geographer, had similar reservations about 'dabbling with the emotions of youngsters'. Both seemed to have strongly resisted a new perspective that they felt was remote from their current area of competence and interest. Construed thus, their reaction, all of us in the group tended to agree, was at least comparable to that of some of our resistant pupils: 'I know nothing about this; I could be exposed, made to feel daft here. Better to keep a low profile or opt out.' Or, 'I'm not interested in this, it's not worth giving time to it.'

A useful tool for examining our reaction to change (and what is teaching but the management of carefully planned change in our pupils?) has been elaborated by the management consultant Elliot-Kemp, of Helios International. Change always involves movement from where we are to a new position, and the challenge to the manager from the managed will constantly be, 'But why should I move?' This was the reaction of my two newspaper-reading colleagues, and my task as a teacher (a manager of their exposure to a new perspective) was to reply constructively to the question.

A ————————————————————▶ B

Safe, competent,   Risky, incompetent,
comfortable   uncomfortable

Figure 3.1 A model of change applicable to learning.

Elliot-Kemp suggests that the model outlined in Figure 3.1 represents a simple way to understand a key element in our attitude to change. The move from point A to point B, which represents any change we undertake, inevitably takes us from the known to the unknown. Our starting point is the familiar, the comfortable, the practised. The point to which we are invited to journey is new, unfamiliar and thus uncomfortable. There is a real sense in which every invitation to learn is an invitation to become voluntarily incompetent for a while. The newspaper-reading colleagues were being invited to leave their practised expertise in geography or mathematics to reach out for the unfamiliarity of a new curricular dimension; there was undoubtedly a feeling of possible exposure, and a self-protective refusal to take the risk. That happens to our pupils – and to us as we undertake the risky business of professional development. For any of us to take the risk involved in learning, we need to feel safe.

A key question for any teacher (manager of learning) is the learner's cautious challenge, 'Why should I move?' Why, indeed, should a pupil, a participant on a course on responses to challenging pupil behaviour, anyone involved in learning, accept my invitation to risk, to be uncomfortable, to be voluntarily incompetent for a while? As a learner I inevitably pose the question, 'Is it safe enough to take the risks involved in moving?' When I am in a teacher role it is my job to create a reassuring 'safe space' to encourage the learner to take that risk. If I cannot do that there is a powerful tendency in the learner (as in the case of the two teachers mentioned above) to resist, opt out or even sabotage the proffered experience. This resistance often emerges in what is called 'disruptive behaviour', and there are clearly occasions when *any* learner will feel moved to engage in such self-protective strategies.

The analysis is elegantly simple, and finds ample research support in self-theory, management and organizational psychology, group dynamics and counselling psychology (Burns, 1979, 1982; Handy, 1985; Cooper, 1981; Argyle, 1983; Rogers, 1965, 1983; Sprinthall, 1981). It merits the closest attention from us, both as teachers and learners, leaving with us the task of converting the theoretical analysis into practice.

We can find in Argyle's (1983, 1988) work a distinction between two types of leadership. As 'leaders', we teachers, it appears, present to our pupils two different and complementary styles of leading. Both are important if effective change is to occur. They are described as *task* leadership and *social* leadership. In my experience, teachers are generally highly skilled task leaders, well able to communicate to pupils the task leader's message: I know this field, am expert, well trained. Follow me with confidence and I'll make sure we achieve our objectives. It is rare to come across a teacher of French who lacks language skills or a chemist who is ignorant of science. We are, generally, well trained in our subjects, know our syllabuses, are able to present our materials in an accessible way to pupils. Managers in other areas – commerce, industry or the public services – have developed an increasing awareness that important though task competence is (i.e. the ability to do the specific job), it is even more important in promoting change to be able to motivate those with whom we are working. The task – for us the academic development of our pupils – cannot proceed until we win their cooperation. It is in seeking to do this that social leadership ability becomes important. The competent social leader is able to give a motivating context, within which the task of changing is more likely to occur. He or she does this by the ability to convey a second communication alongside the task-focused message. Not only, 'I know this field, follow me', but also, 'in pursuing this task you will not be humiliated or hurt, diminished or damaged. You will be looked after, enhanced and valued'. It seems almost too idealistic, and I must confess that it provokes the odd snort from the battle-hardened veterans of some particularly difficult schools. There will always be a rump of pupils who fail to respond to teacher attempts to create respecting environments, but it does seem to be managerially unimaginative to allow a small fraction of pupils to govern our relationships with the huge majority. We need to devise contingency strategies to deal with those challenges within a generally collaborative ethos. Such responses will be examined in Chapter 5.

The weary reaction of those teachers who have borne the heat of the day can jolt the confidence of those who want to move beyond mere control to a more productive relationship with reluctant learners. It is, therefore, reassuring to find one of the major oil companies promoting its interpersonally aware style of management; not, we can be pretty sure, out of some wishy-washy desire to appear noble. It is quite simply that in all endeavours the weight of the research evidence suggests that we get better results from collaborative, respecting management than from punitive management.

A key feature of this text must be an attempt to delineate ways in which such a managerial style might be developed and used. To what extent is my own, and my school's, management of pupil behaviour infused with highly developed social leadership skills? To move beyond this brief outline of aspects of effective management to effective practice there follow initial exercises which take some of the key concepts discussed above into account.

Practical work

The size of group envisaged for this and later practical work is not a central issue. I have worked with school-based colleagues with this material in groups that have varied in size from twelve to ninety. The important thing is to use the ideas in a way that fits your own situation.

The issue of pupil behaviour is a very hot potato. Everyone has strong views, anxieties, feelings of professional inadequacy. A vital initial task is to create the 'safe space' for participants that will help all in the group to feel comfortable; it needs to be fun, relaxing and accepting. If it lacks these qualities, we can lock ourselves into the defensive positions described earlier. It cannot be overemphasized that, in INSET as in the school classroom, real progress relates closely to the social leadership skills of the group leader. The examples below, and throughout the book, cannot be used prescriptively. Each group will move at its own pace and depth. Given that the teacher, deploying both task and social leadership skills, is constantly trying to balance degree of challenge and degree of support, alternative activities with varying degrees of challenge are offered. The Appendix offers a sample 12-hour programme, which draws on activities from the whole book.

Activity 1: an ice-breaking exercise (approx. 5 minutes)
It would be a waste not to tap all of the experience, insight and creativity of this group. On INSET and initial training courses, time limits often lead us into the false economy of bypassing the talent already present in the group. To avoid that, we need somehow to establish an atmosphere of mutual respect and openness to the wide range of different values that infuse our ideas about pupil behaviour. I'd like us to work in groups of six. Can I ask you, then, to find five colleagues with, as closely as possible, the same colour of eyes as yourself?

This exercise has an element of risk, but it also has a jokey ability to stretch social boundaries, generate chatter and a sense of fun. More seriously, it puts the issue of 'safe' risk-taking on to the agenda immediately. Its main purpose is climate creation and grouping, but it contains a rich vein of learning about safety in new situations. The group may wish to discuss these questions:

How did I feel doing the exercise? initially? in the middle? finally?

Did some of us feel more exposed than others?

What happened to intensify or reduce that feeling of exposure?

Are there any lessons here applicable to pupil learning?

Alternative ice-breaker (approx. 15 minutes)

Can I ask you to form groups of six? Will each of you draw to mind your 'classroom nightmare', the incident that has you waking up, terrified, muttering, 'Oh, no! Not that.' It may be something that has happened to you, or that you fear might happen.

Having drawn to mind such an incident, take it in turns to recount it to the other colleagues in your group. (These incidents can be written up and used as case material at a later point in the course.)

This exercise helps to establish that all of us face the challenge of difficult pupils. It gives permission and a forum in which to recount difficulties and anxieties, which many young teachers say is hard to find in school. It also permits us to think up 'worst case' scenarios, in an environment which gives time for reflection. Colleagues become very involved in this initial sharing, which also helps to establish an open and supportive climate.

Activity 2: agenda-setting (approx. 45 minutes)

There is little point in a teacher answering questions that do not address the learner's concerns. We need some strategy to allow the group to declare clearly, 'These are the things that I'd like to work on.' To some extent, the 'classroom nightmare' exercise has begun the process. The following exercise deepens and extends it.

The task here is to spend 10–15 minutes producing a personal heraldic shield that, as in real heraldry, gives some clue to some of the central elements that make you who you are, from a professional point of view. (Prepare an overhead projector slide for display; this can be based on Figure 3.2.)

In space 1 draw, write or represent in some way 'My greatest fear or anxiety in the issue of pupil behaviour'. It can be anything at all, personal, organizational, interprofessional. Be as honest as you can.

In space 2, similarly, represent 'My greatest achievement or success in the area of pupil behaviour'. Let your mind roam to any distant or recent success.

In space 3 represent any personal characteristic that helps you in this challenging area of teaching. Do not be modest! (Humour, toughness, gentleness, warmth, fairness, or something quite different.)

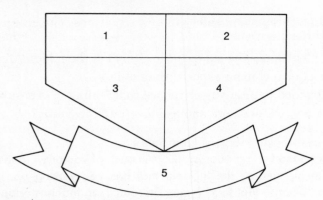

Figure 3.2 Heraldic shield exercise on pupil behaviour.

In space 4 represent some element in your personality which reduces your effectiveness with difficult pupils and which you would like to change. Be adventurous.

In space 5 write in a personal motto that sums up your view of the current situation *vis-à-vis* pupil behaviour.

(During this exercise the group is producing a cumulative programme:

Fears, anxieties, major challenges;

Ways of responding successfully, strategies that work;

A wide repertoire of intra- and interpersonal traits that might help;

Personal programmes for change, exploration.

The collaborative dimension of the exercise is powerful in its ability to offer new, wider visions of what is possible, gentle contrasts of differing values, harder challenges about practice that must occur within that safe and mutually respecting climate.)

Group leaders will have to structure the data drawn in a way that makes its use possible. Are colleagues identifying task or social leadership issues, are they concerned primarily about pre-emptive climate creation or response to critical incidents, are the key issues intra- or interpersonal, is the central issue organizational?

Given the risk taken in this kind of sharing, it is essential that the responses become the heart of the professional development programme. We cannot say, 'Thank you' and then move back to our pre-set agenda.

The purpose of the initial part of the exercise is to give an opportunity for reflection and self-analysis. It is important not to 'crowd' participants, and to emphasize that the degree of sharing of material is entirely each person's decision. It is a 'Where am I starting from?' exercise.

The second part of the exercise is an invitation to each person to talk the rest of the group of six through the shield he or she has produced. Again, freedom not to disclose the material needs to be stressed, with a parallel statement of the insights that can be gained from the opening sharing. (It is frequently at this point that a degree of real honesty about fears, styles of relating to pupils, skills and absence of skills appears. This 'honest material' – no façades or pretending – is precious and its continuation depends on its being valued, respected and used from the outset.)

When all six participants have had an opportunity to speak about the themes on their shield, the full group leader might try to draw together two sets of material, as follows:

(a) What major themes have emerged in this group?
    Are there any surprises about issues that emerged?
    Do you detect any major clashes in attitudes or values?
    Can we continue on a basis of real, mutual respect on value
        difference?

(b) So far what *feelings*, *values* have I experienced in this group?
    Anxiety, fear, anger, frustration, pleasure, comradeship, threat, or
        other things.
    Is it easy to answer the questions above? Honestly?
    How would you describe the climate of this group? Supportive,
        threatening?
    How would I like it to change?
    What insights into pupil learning can I take from my experience in
        the group?

Activity 3: teaching that harms – or helps
    The emphasis given to the effect of group climate on task performance rests on a body of evidence that can be traced back to Triplett, who worked at the end of the last century (Cartwright and Zanders, 1968), and through to the most modern theories of management (Everard, 1984; Handy, 1985). If this has any basis, there are clear implications for our own INSET work and work with pupils. The following exercise adds an individual dimension to the abundant research.

    Would each group member draw to mind from the past some teacher, about whom you would say, 'That teacher damaged me in some way; hurt me, reduced my confidence and effectiveness'? In other words, draw to mind from your past a teacher who had a destructive effect. Having done that, working with one other person in the group, imagine your partner *is* that harmful teacher. You have one minute to say to that teacher anything you would like to have said all those years ago, but dared not. Make it personal – not, 'S/he used to hurt me when ...', but 'You used to hurt me when ...' No hitting is allowed.

When both partners have had a turn, collect on a flip-chart the full group's perceptions of the characteristics of 'the destructive teacher'. Keep them for later use.

The parallel task takes advantage of the fact that most of us have also experienced a totally different kind of teacher, who was special, helpful, offering us visions of our potential that were enormously facilitative. Draw to mind such a teacher and do the same exercise as before, this time collecting on the flip-chart the characteristics of the special teacher.

Remember, be personal. Not, 'S/he helped me when/because ...', but 'You were special for me because/when ...'

It has been my consistent experience doing this exercise with slight contextual variations (with GPs, nurses, commercial managers, social workers, even HM inspectors, indeed with anyone involved in interpersonal contact as part of their work) that professionals consistently identify social leadership factors over task leadership factors. It seems that our experience of being learners does coincide with the research findings. Destructive capacity as a teacher (and the consequent pupil reaction of some form of self-defence) correlates strongly with an absence of social leadership skills, while the ability to have a powerful and positive influence on pupils relates to the presence of such skills (McGuiness and Craggs, 1986).

We need both abilities in order to prosper as teachers, but our ability as subject specialists will fail without the foundational ability to relate.

SOME TEACHER RESPONSES TO THE FOREGOING

It is important for the INSET or ITT (initial teacher training) trainer not simply to elicit colleague disclosure about pupil behaviour, but to use it. Since each group is unique, reactions to the exercises will vary, but a number of fairly consistent concerns emerge with some regularity. It may be helpful to list some of these as a means of making an outline preparation for the group discussion.

The shield

It is a little surprising in view of the Elton Report's comment, 'our evidence is that attacks are rare in schools.... We also find that teachers do not see attacks as their major problem.... Teachers were most concerned about the cumulative effects of disruption ... caused by trivial but persistent misbehaviour' (DES, 1989: 11,3), to find teachers on INSET courses and students in training identifying as major fears violence, sexually charged incidents, chaos, i.e. a class-wide breakdown of order, as well as other colleagues' perception of them as incompetent. The case material we will consider in later chapters puts flesh on the bones of these anxieties. Despite the apparent inconsistency between the Elton findings and the expressed fears of teachers I think the explanation is that Elton is speaking of occurrences and the teachers of fears about what *could* occur. The fears are real, if unfounded, and trainers must allow them to be expressed and worked on. In the initial stages teachers will often try to outdo each other in identifying classroom challenges. Classroom crisis does occur and must be prepared for.

In terms of sharing their successes, participants have in the past identified such things as establishing a relationship with a difficult adolescent, overcoming fear, improving the ability to maintain eye contact and becoming more confident. Each needs to be talked about, turned over and studied. It may be noticeable that the successes involve socioemotional developments rather than some new academic skill, and this is worth drawing out. It will be a constant feature of increasing managerial skills that colleagues will grow in the awareness that such skills flourish in an atmosphere characterized by 'good relationships with mutual respect between teachers and pupils' (DES, 1987). This is not some idealistic velleity, it is a managerial objective to be assiduously pursued.

In responding to the invitation to analyse positive and negative characteristics of self, group members are engaging in highly professional and courageous work. While the self-audit is relatively common in the business world, it is still relatively rare in the world of education. Again, such an analysis will occur only in a respecting and supportive environment. A willingness to say 'I am a cold person', 'find it difficult to relate to others', 'am shy', even 'I don't like children' (all examples drawn from recent INSET) needs to be supported with respect, attention and not a little humour. I remember doing some professional development with a group of psychiatric nurses, one of whom reduced the class to helpless and relieved complicit laughter when she said her biggest professional weakness was a recurring desire to take her patients out, one at a time, and drop them into the nearby river. It was important, not because we had flushed out a deranged nurse but because one nurse had expanded our boundaries of disclosure by sharing her 'unthinkable', unprofessional fantasies and we felt relieved that a climate was being established in which we could be more fully ourselves.

We do have strengths as well as failings and the sharing of them is no less important in self-audit than the examples identified above. Teachers do declare themselves to be warm, caring, understanding, and also, in slight, productive contrast, firm disciplinarians: tough, just, having high standards. The deeper layers of these concepts need to be explored, since our decisions and actions are influenced at least as much by feeling and value as by logic and reason.

The fourth element of the shield allows individuals to produce an initial programme for self-development. Where one colleague may wish to improve pupil behaviour in her French classes by finding more engaging material (a task leadership objective), another may identify improving the ability to relate to adolescents as a goal (a social leadership objective). By this early sharing group members will also gain new perspectives from colleagues on the course, and a list of necessary qualities for effective teaching will be gradually, cumulatively developed.

The motto (in space 5) is frequently treated humorously. 'Hang 'em and flog 'em', said one shield; 'Nil carborundum' said another. Back to the half-serious humour of the nurse. The relaxing effect of tutorial acceptance of such frivolity (real acceptance, not gritted-teeth acceptance) makes the contrasting mottoes of colleagues who opted to remain serious all the more influential. 'Pupils are people' is a productive contrast only if the other items are accepted without demur.

By this time the group is beginning to become cohesive and genuinely exploratory. The facilitator/leader needs to watch constantly for interventions that could destroy the safety of members of the group. If a destructive element occurs, don't dodge it, use it. Bear in mind the suggestion at the outset that the group agree to 'use our own learning as a reference point for pupil learning'. It may be helpful now to use an example of such 'immediate feedback' from a recent course.

The group was working on a case study in which a PGCE student had gone into a fourth-year class on teaching practice, for the first time. I had asked the group to look at what advice they would give, as experienced teachers, to the student in the light of what occurred. The student, a geographer, had taken some maps into the class to be distributed at an appropriate moment. When the time came, he said to a fifteen-year-old girl, 'Will you give everyone one of these?', handing her the maps. 'F*** off, you, you're just a student, you can't boss me around,' was the reply. As with the readers of this text, the group evinced all manner of reactions – outrage, curiosity, shock, concern – the incident was being run through the twenty participants' individual, professional filters. Of course there is no 'right' response; we were about to discover the essentially idiosyncratic response to adolescent challenge. Little did I realize that we would draw from our own reaction some key lessons about disruption.

Mary, four years into the profession and highly regarded by her colleagues, volunteered: 'Well, I think I'd say something along the lines of, "When I come into this classroom I will treat everyone with respect and courtesy and I'd like to be treated in the same way." Then I'd give the maps to someone else and say, "Would you mind?"' Before I could react, a rumbling, almost contemptuous belly-laugh grew to my left. 'Young lady,' the laugh vocalized, 'if you did that in my school they would laugh in your face and eat you alive.' I privately wondered where on earth they would learn such behaviour! I did notice that Mary had flushed angrily at John's (aged fifty-eight, senior teacher in charge of probationers, and highly thought of by his colleagues) comment.

I intervened: 'Can I change our focus for a moment, away from the case to this group. We will all be reacting differently to the exchange between John and Mary; it may be helpful to consider that for a few minutes. Mary, can I ask you to say how you *feel* at the moment? Don't argue your view, just concentrate on how you feel.'

'I feel angry,' she said. 'I know my eyes are moist, but they are tears of anger at that patronizing comment. He's trying to de-skill me. And what about the "young lady" bit. Where's that coming from?'

John was quite taken aback. 'You're a bit sensitive, aren't you?', he said insensitively. Some of the group were clearly processing the exchange in a very effective way. I asked for other contributions, and received ideas that spanned a continuum from Mary's idea to John's suggestions that he would 'have that girl by the hair of the head, drag her out of the classroom, and up to the head's office so we could have the parents in'. I commented that in facing a comparable challenge as a young teacher in Chicago I had, as a terrified automatic pilot, tried a strategy not unlike the one Mary had outlined. John was not impressed. 'Don't give us all that guff about the States,' he said with all the support I was beginning to expect from him! 'Hang on a second, John,' I said. 'We're trying here to do some professional sharing and you seem intent on drying us up. We all need some positive response if we're to continue sharing ideas.'

'I can't believe how touchy you all are,' was the reply. I knew by now that the exchanges were not taking place in a vacuum. Rather, the group was doing a managerial audit on the effect of John's comments on us as a group.

'OK,' I said, 'let's get back to the case material. Can we role-play a couple of the suggested responses, just to see how they feel? John, can you run us through yours – I'll be the pupil, but go easy if you're going to pull my hair.'

We arranged a mini-classroom and began. I repeated the pupil's fierce refusal to cooperate.

'What did you say, young lady?', said John in disbelief.

'What do you mean, "What did I say"?', I role-played back.

'You know very well what I mean,' roared John, advancing on me, and quite enjoying this moment of stardom.

'You're too f****** sensitive,' I fired back, tensing my scalp against the expected onslaught. It did not arrive. John stared me in disbelief, the group laughed, John picked up his papers and stalked out to our stunned silence.

Someone said, 'It was just getting interesting.' Uneasy laughter. I had to confess that though the odd pupil had done a runner on me, I'd never had a teacher do it. 'What do you want to do about it?' I asked. 'We must have him back,' was the reply. 'We'd really got to something quite unusual in INSET. It's the meatiest encounter I've ever experienced on a course.'

We decided to write as a group to John at his school, repeating in detail some of the views we had heard expressed, and saying that we hoped he would rejoin the group the following week. He did, and in a highly professional way analysed the whole process of the previous week. 'I've been at this teaching game for nearly thirty-six years, without thinking much about it, and last week you lot held up a mirror for me. I wasn't too keen on what I saw.'

An initial antipathy towards John was replaced by a genuine admiration. Like all of us a product of his time, his training and his experience, he had responded with real courage to the invitation to change. He was at first very resistant to the idea of moving from the safe, familiar and practised in the direction of new perspectives and new practices. He laid his values on the line, disclosed feelings, tested new skills. How had it occurred?

Like most groups we had begun to test the reactions of our peers to check out what level of risk felt appropriate. Is this a 'play safe' group? Just keep your head down, say nothing controversial and get off to the pub as soon as it finishes. This, or something very similar, is the initial theme of my pupils in my classroom. As the group facilitator I had to do what all teachers do: let my class know that it is OK to experiment with ideas, be creative, even be outrageous in the quest for learning. Mary tried gently to share an idea; no great insight, a tentative, group-probing sort of a foray. She soon learned the risks involved in putting her head above the parapet. Sniper John got her with his first shot – 'young lady ...'. In a sense it was brilliant sabotage, downing the person and the idea at the same time. Beyond that, John's own discomfort with the idea of exploration was protected as, almost visibly, others in the group curled up into self-protective postures: 'My God, if he does that to Mary, what will he do to me if I say what my views are?' In the flash of an eye the group can be locked into playing safe, with uncreative, plodding responses.

Mary, too, showed great courage in returning to the fray at my invitation. Yes, she was angry; yes, she perceived the latent sexism and brought it to the surface for analysis; no, she would not be de-skilled, and wanted to continue the risk-taking. Thanks to her, the group was reassured that it *was* OK to put oneself on the line. The behaviour of others in the group, on which I have given little detail, was also influential, in that they voiced, in various ways, support for Mary – not necessarily for her position, but at least for her willingness to risk that position to the full group. A detailed analysis of group dynamics and non-verbal influence is presented in Chapter 6.

The final element in the drama, in which John and I began the role play, was not at all planned. It couldn't be. I found myself wondering how I could get John to empathize with the group he had attacked for its excessive 'sensitivity'. I hoped he would set on one side what Piaget refers to in children as the 'egocentric' view and embrace a more accepting view: what Rogers describes as 'empathic understanding', accepting, working with and genuinely valuing the perspectives of those with whom we work. All progress in learning is retarded when that ability is absent in the teacher. When it is there, the sky is the limit.

This unusual account is worth sharing because it emphasizes both the challenge of carefully analysing group climate and its usefulness.

DESTRUCTIVE TEACHERS AND HELPFUL TEACHERS

I have examined this exercise at length elsewhere (McGuiness, 1988). It is an exercise that invites participants in a tangential way to search for the fundamental characteristics of good and bad teachers. While I in no way wish to devalue the academic skills of teachers, it is significant that members of all professions with an interpersonal dimension highlight socio-emotional qualities. As one GP said to the group after doing the exercise, 'It's not that diagnostic skill and pharmacological ability aren't important. It's just that without the interpersonal capabilities you're thrashing around in the dark.' I wish a teacher had said that.

Some readers may be thinking that we have not yet got to grips with pupil behaviour. I hope that the huge majority will have accepted my central opening thesis: that pupil behaviour is a management issue, that management is a creative activity which of its nature transcends neat, predictable solutions, and that effective managerial activities can occur only in a climate of mutual respect; finally, that to learn about managing others, I can find a rich vein of material in my own response to being managed.

The next chapter continues the important idea that to help improve pupil behaviour I need to spend some time examining my own contribution to the interaction. Who is this 'I' that I take into the classroom?

CHAPTER 4

Decisions of value

Honest foundations

The previous chapter emphasized the importance of the climate of the working environment. A punitive, ego-defensive, distant teacher will produce cautious, ego-defensive, resistant behaviour from the pupils. It may well be that such 'non-problematic' behaviour by pupils is regarded by some as desirable. One of the operating rules of the late Roman Empire, referring to citizenry under that punitive regime, was 'Let them hate, provided that they also fear.' Few teachers would want to propose such a climate, but it is evident that there is a considerable range of views about relationships in the classroom within the profession. We need look no further than the earlier discussion of the differing approaches of John and Mary in facing the swearing pupil.

That contrast, in practical terms, draws attention to a basic distinction in our possible responses to pupil challenge. It is the different priority given in varying contexts to the issues of *control* and *education*. I would like to suggest that in the final analysis we are not faced by a problem of control; the real challenge to the teacher is to create the kind of context within which learning can take place. There is a sense in which an emphasis on control *per se* destroys the educational endeavour. Of course, there are occasions when all our skill and energy is directed towards control (for example when misbehaviour in a laboratory becomes dangerous). At that point, we momentarily discard the educator's role and become guardians of public order, or policemen. Such occasions arise and we must respond to them, but when order and safety are restored the good teacher uses the incident as a learning opportunity for the pupils. From our point of view, in consideration of pupil behaviour it can be a useful element in our self-scrutiny to try to locate ourselves on the controller–educator continuum. In the example at the end of the previous chapter we could say that John tends towards the 'control' end of the continuum, and Mary towards the 'education' end. They have different priorities, differing values. John says, 'How can I get back on top of this situation?' where Mary asks, 'What learning for my pupils can I extract here?' It is not a dichotomy; it is a difference of priority that flows from a different hierarchy of values. John is committed to educate, just as Mary is committed to order.

So we arrive at the important issues of values. It is not strange that in analysing the psychology of how humans make decisions the literature emphasizes the nodal role of our value system. It is a literature that is well used in the media and advertising, where it helps the advertiser to direct our decision-making, but it is given scant attention by educators. The American psychologist Gelatt (1962) produced a model of how we arrive at decisions. Why do John and Mary, facing the same incident, arrive at different operational decisions? Gelatt's model may help both to draw our attention to and to explain another area that requires our attention, before we go on to detailed case material from classrooms.

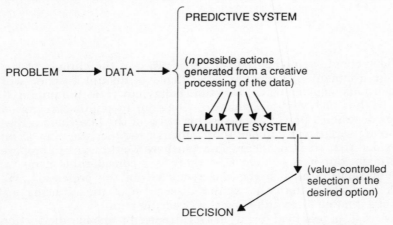

Figure 4.1 A model of how we make decisions (after Gelatt, 1962).

The model (Figure 4.1) suggests that when we are faced with the need to make a decision, the challenge is construed as a problem. We assemble the maximum data available, relevant to the problem, drawing on as many sources as seems appropriate. We then pass this database through what Gelatt calls our 'predictive system', our logical capacity to generate a wide range of possible responses to the problem. Given this challenge and these data, what courses of action are open to me? Our creativity is a variable here, the ability to think divergently, so it is useful to do some exercises that help develop this capacity. It is worth mentioning that divergent thinking is intellectual risk-taking, and that it is all too easy, as in any learning situation, to stifle it (cf. the stifling effect of the hypercritical comments of John).

At this point we tend to think that the analysis is complete. We have generated n possible responses to this problem. Gelatt, however, insists that the analysis must go on to the next stage: given the range of possible actions, what process leads me to choose this one rather than any of the others? The challenging thesis of Gelatt is that however much we try to cling to some concept that gives primacy to logic ('I judge this to be the most appropriate action'), we arrive eventually at a set of criteria for making that judgement which are an implicit statement of values. For Gelatt, values lie at the core of our decision-making process, and must be considered by the professional decision-maker: not to do so would be to allow an influential element of professional activity to operate randomly. The final element of the process is to pass the range of possible actions through an 'evaluative system' which, on the basis of the person's own values, will lead to the selection of a course of action.

If responding to the challenge of pupil behaviour is a managerial problem, and if the heart of management is decision-making, and if, further, our decisions are value founded, then we must pay some attention to the question of values at school, classroom and interpersonal levels.

School-based colleagues are sometimes initially annoyed at my claim that the central issue in pupil behaviour is not one of control. It was comforting for me to find both the Elton Report (DES, 1989) and the DES document (1987) giving prominence to the idea explored by Rutter *et al.* (1979), that 'the ethos or climate of a school is central to establishing and maintaining high standards of behaviour'. Comforting though it is to see the coinciding views of research and official reports, the hard-pressed classroom teacher remains suspicious that the 'experts' will sit on the sidelines of the really tough cases, while pontificating about the values of 'ethos'. I hope that is not my position, and want to emphasize my commitment to orderly learning environments. However, it does seem to be professionally desirable not to resort to mere control before it is necessary.

It may help to analyse my basic response to pupil misbehaviour by positioning it on a value continuum (Figure 4.2). The continuum is not a

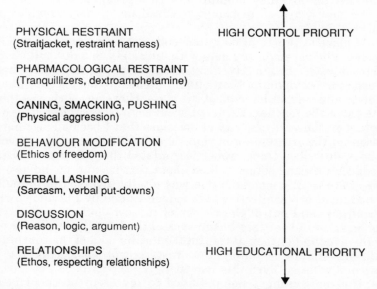

PHYSICAL RESTRAINT   HIGH CONTROL PRIORITY
(Straitjacket, restraint harness)

PHARMACOLOGICAL RESTRAINT
(Tranquillizers, dextroamphetamine)

CANING, SMACKING, PUSHING
(Physical aggression)

BEHAVIOUR MODIFICATION
(Ethics of freedom)

VERBAL LASHING
(Sarcasm, verbal put-downs)

DISCUSSION
(Reason, logic, argument)

RELATIONSHIPS   HIGH EDUCATIONAL PRIORITY
(Ethos, respecting relationships)

Figure 4.2 A value-tendency continuum, from control to educational priority.

dichotomy; at different times and in different circumstances I will position myself differently. Equally, I will find that my value tendency will
vary from that of my colleagues; we are different people with varying
perceptions and talents. The usefulness of the continuum is that it establishes the idea of range of response. It runs from a total preoccupation
with and commitment to control, to a total preoccupation with and commitment to educating.

At the control end, I would place John's initial reaction to the swearing
pupil (see Chapter 3, p. 26). He is intent on crushing the discourtesy,
punishing it, and will do so with little or no thought for the broader
issues. High on his value hierarchy is control, respect for authority, his
sense of dignity. He might also find, just below the surface, values to do
with gender, which intensify his sense of outrage. It is certainly not the
task of an INSET leader to change colleagues' values, but it does seem
appropriate to provide opportunities for everyone to raise those values to
a level of awareness where they can be examined and *consciously*
embraced.

Mary's response seems to be more central. She appears both to want to
restore order and to use the incident for its educational potential. She
does not condone the discourtesy, but she does make sure that the whole
class learns from it. Her high values seem to be those of learning, interpersonal respect, and a sufficiently high sense of personal worth for it not
to be threatened by the incident. I have no wish to make an invidious
comparison between the two approaches. Indeed, to do so could severely
damage the hard-won feeling of safety in the group, as I almost found to
my cost when John left us. The key is to leave critical analysis to the
individual: 'what are my underlying values, how do they influence my
decision-making, are they helpful or counterproductive, do I see in my
colleagues new ways of responding, based on a more complex value
system?'

I would place at the 'total educator' end of the continuum a probationary teacher who asked for my help with lab safety in a difficult class. We
agreed to co-teach, though, given my incompetence as a scientist, her role
was much more demanding than mine. I decided to keep a careful eye on
the climate and safety elements of the class. However, such was the task
competence of the teacher, her mastery of chemistry and ability to communicate it to the vast majority of her class that I became fascinated by
her lesson on the fractioning of coal. She distilled a number of volatile
substances, described their properties, related them to everyday items;
she produced tars and solids; talked about textiles and medicines. I and
the class were totally engaged. She was totally involved in her subject,
the embodiment of the effective task leader. Suddenly I became aware of
a smell of gas, and out of the corner of my eye noticed a pupil coolly
turning on all of the gas taps at the back of the lab. The teacher was still
totally involved in her task at the 'total educator' end of the continuum. I
was heavily and immediately into my 'control mode, flinging open
windows and yelling, 'Turn that gas off!'

Thus, the continuum is not intended to represent an ideal mode of
teaching. It simply reminds us that we have access to a wide range of

responses, that require us to choose intelligently and flexibly, according to our own values, abilities and the circumstances that face us. Using it I can subject my classroom behaviour to a searching scrutiny, so that it becomes more deliberate and the values that underpin it become more on the surface and accessible. Equally, it permits us to discuss within a structure the variation of values that can undermine consistency in the application of school policy. The DES document (1987) speaks of 'clear priorities collectively agreed ... a communal sense of purpose', yet I regularly find that in preparing school policy documents on pupil behaviour no systematic exploration of the value range among school staff has been carried out. Heads can presume a consensual dimension which in reality does not exist.

The continuum is not a fantastical invention. All of the control approaches described on it have been, or are still, available to us as teachers. As a head of a special unit I might want a restraint harness, but it is unlikely (though perhaps tempting!) that the ordinary teacher will use a straitjacket. The point is that our reaction to the different strategies is a useful indicator of our priorities. How do I react to the idea of tranquillizing disruptives? In the USA and UK during the 1960s and 1970s some disruptive pupils were diagnosed as hyperactive, and tranquillized or given dextroamphetamine, a mild stimulant used in adults to control depression or senile behaviour (Schrag and Divoky, 1981). What about caning, now illegal, but still part of the mythology of teaching? Do I regret its abolition? Is my reaction nostalgia, or a carefully formulated, objective-driven position? There is, after all, evidence that pain is an effective, though short-term, behaviour modifier. Does the teacher who regrets the loss of the cane hold on to residual, physical control strategies (leg-smacking in the primary school, aggressive pushing in the secondary school) that jar with school policy? My own area of unease occurs when I examine the way in which I slip easily into sarcasm and verbal bullying. What value system allows me to do that? Can I, do I want to change it? The use of behaviour modification techniques raises ethical issues that must be faced. Challenging, too, is the use of reason, logic, argument – inevitably attractive to the reasonable, logical person, but we need to ask to what extent they provide access to 'attitude-based' misbehaviour, such as racism, sexism or religious intolerance.

All of these examples offer themselves to us as responses to pupils' behavioural challenges. The professional's task is to select deliberately a way of responding which permits teaching to occur and is consonant with his or her own carefully formulated value system. If all I want is to control (and as we have seen, that can be the case), then I need to decide that openly: if, as will be the case most of the time, I see order as a means to the end of teaching, then I am accepting the difficult challenge of pursuing task and social leadership at the same time.

We take into all our encounters with pupils a dynamic set of values which strongly influence our interaction with them. Whether we are aware of the influence or not, they also affect the way in which we individually decide what constitutes disruptive behaviour, and how serious it is. This, too, has implications for formulations of school policy.

What Mr Cane sees as 'totally unacceptable impertinence', Miss Hope will consider 'socially gauche, but eager participation'. Gelatt's insistence on the key role played by our value system in decision-making means that often unexamined attitudes towards authority, sexuality and gender, class and accent, hygiene, academic excellence, courtesy and social skill can lead us to unintentionally exaggerate (or minimize) an incident to accommodate our own values. Unless there is a school acceptance of the need to air this dissonance, and a forum in which to do so, a subtle and insidious process will leave us far from the HMI (1987) exhortation to ensure that 'clear priorities are *cooperatively* pursued' (emphasis added).

The Elton Report (DES, 1989), in appendices F1 to F4, offers helpful examples of a variety of such agreements. It is clear, from the examples the Report offers, that schools do vary in the priorities they choose.

It is tempting to regard consultations as a waste of precious time. The use of coercive management styles has the attraction that it is quick, but in the longer term the coercive manager may lose time in combating the uncooperative response of the coerced. Caldwell and Miskow's (1984) analysis of managerial style suggests that joint problem-solving leads to high-quality output, but that it is time-consuming in the short term.

Finally, what can the busy manager or fed-up colleagues do about the value maverick? – the person who wants the pupils to call him 'George', or in contrast, who wants to bring back hanging! If we succumb to the temptation to crush or ridicule that person, we are making possible all the dangers of coercive management. We can impose a silence on the dissident at the cost of long-term non-cooperation. If we accept dissidence openly and respectfully we leave the 'safe ethos' intact. We can use the maverick view as a helpful critique of the organization's orthodoxy. It can become, genuinely, a refiner of practice. Of course, there is an important professional corollary of the organization's respect for dissidence, which is that, once agreed, there can be no sabotage of the 'cooperatively agreed' position.

And so to practice. Values are by their nature personal and the exercises need to be honestly, but sensitively, handled. They may seem remote from the practice of classroom management skills, but values are so ingrained in us that it is sometimes useful, initially, to do a bit of digging away from the familiar.

Activity 1: consensus and dissonance in values (45 minutes)

This exercise is designed to allow a group to explore value variation, its effect on group relations and possible effects on organizational behaviour. (I was first introduced to a variation of it by John Storey, then of the Schools Council, and have come across different versions of it. Like all games, it belongs to everybody.)

The group leader can either read out or prepare copies of the following story. The task of the group, initially, is to listen carefully.

'The SS *Value Laden* sank in the South Pacific, while on a cruise. Sadly, there was considerable loss of life, with only five passengers surviving. They scrambled ashore on to two separate islands, about half a mile apart. [See Figure 4.3, which can be reproduced on a blackboard or flip-chart for the group.]

Ann
Brian
Colin

Dave
Eric

Kulova

Tanata

Figure 4.3 Value exercise, SS *Value Laden*: consensus/dissonance.

'On the atoll of Kulova the survivors were Ann, Brian and Colin (ABC, for ease of recall), and on the island of Tanata there were Dave and Eric (D and E). Of course, all were greatly relieved to have survived, but unfortunately, Ann and Dave had been on a honeymoon cruise, and now found themselves separated by half a mile of shark-infested sea. Both were very sad. Suddenly, Ann remembered that Brian had not swum ashore like the rest of them, he arrived in a small dinghy that he had managed to secure on abandoning ship. Elated, Ann asked him to help. "I don't want the boat," she said, "but would you just row me across to Dave?"

'Brian smiled an evil smile. "Of course," he said. "No problem. I'm sure we can come to some arrangement about the fare."

' "But that's silly," said Ann. "You know that none of us managed to salvage anything from the wreck."

'Brian smiled again. "Oh, I think you and I can come to some arrangement about the fare," he said.

'To her horror, Ann realized that she was being blackmailed. What a dreadful choice faced her! Distraught, she paced up and down the beach.

'As she walked, Colin approached and said, "I couldn't help overhearing your conversation with Brian, and I understand your frustration and anger. However, it seems to me that you are faced with a very straight-forward clash of values. You need to weigh the intensity of your wish to be with Dave against the intensity of the antipathy you feel towards Brian's suggestion. I'm sure it feels very difficult, but basically it's a question of choosing the more valued option."

'Ann, after very careful thought, decided to make the tremendous sacrifice to be with Dave — and submitted to Brian's nefarious black-mail...

'The deed done, Brian rapidly rowed Ann across the stretch of water, dropped her on the beach, and rowed swiftly back to his own atoll. Dave had seen the approaching pair with delight, and leapt across the dunes to be with the woman he loved ... After the first moments of joy at the reunion, Ann became serious and said, "Dave, we've always been very straight with each other, and I never want that to change." She proceeded to tell him of the sordid bargain she had struck with Brian to be with him.

'Dave looked dumbstruck. He stepped back from her. "I can't believe that you could do such a thing. How could you? I'm shocked — no, horrified. I feel you've just destroyed something very important. I'm sorry, I just can't bear to be with you."

'Ann was shattered by his reaction. "I did it because I loved you so much. I did it for you." Sadly, they separated, and wandered to different parts of the island.

'Eric, who had overheard the whole exchange, said to Ann, "I would like you to know that I am overwhelmed by the courage and generosity of what you did for Dave. Nothing more. Just that I wouldn't want you to accept Dave's comments without you knowing that I see what you did as an act of heroism."'

The group now has a very simple task. Would you write down, individually and without reference to colleagues, the names of the five characters in the story *in the order in which you like them*? No deep evaluation, no checking with colleagues — just your immediate reaction. It may help to be reminded that Ann wants to be with her new husband, and has to strike a sordid bargain with Brian, the boatman. Colin tells her clearly that her challenge is a simple value clash that can be resolved in those terms. Dave is the rejecting husband, who is horrified by his wife's act. Eric sees Ann as a heroine. You may feel that you have insufficient information as a basis on which to choose, but consider the ease with which we can say, 'Oh! I don't like him/her' after the briefest of encounters. Deep values operate with great speed.

Share your choices with a partner, if possible of the opposite sex. Don't change your order. Discuss the implicit values that underpin your choice. What led to you choose Ann, Brian, Colin, Dave or Eric? Honesty, courage, caution, sexual or gender values, empathy, power, logic, coolness under pressure, conviction, etc.

Collect your individual choices on to a cumulative flip-chart to initiate the closing discussion on degree of consensus and dissonance, and the implications this can have for our styles of relating to pupils and their subsequent behaviour.

TEACHER REACTION TO THE ABOVE

The exercise surprises many participants because frequently each different character is chosen as favourite by someone. The larger the group, the more likely that is. Even in a small group there is always a considerable range for each character. Ann can be chosen as the favourite by one group member and as the least, or second-least, by another. The choices are powerful indicators of deep values – to be respected, accepted and used to analyse the impact of value dissonance on group cohesion, individual perception and behaviour.

An important element in the processing of this exercise is the analysis, *not* of individual values, but of the reaction we all have to those whose values differ considerably from our own. How does the person who names Dave as his favourite *feel* in the face of a wall of disagreement? How do those teachers with a strong commitment to facing gender issues *feel* towards anyone who puts Ann low down? The exercise often generates strong reactions on the issue of gender. It is an important element of our decision-making on pupil behaviour, and should be used, not ducked. However fierce the discussion, the facilitator needs to let it roll. To do otherwise undermines the notion that values are central in our decision-making.

The open sharing of idiosyncratic views allows colleagues to get into contact with a wider range of value-based responses than their own. A growing awareness can emerge that there are other ways of viewing the problem than our own. There is an unpressured opportunity to compare our perception with that of everyone else, allowing us to broaden our value base, and hence response repertoire.

Activity 2: unacceptable behaviour (15 minutes)

To your undoubted relief, we now turn our attention more concretely to the behaviour of pupils, though still from the perspective of the influence of our values on our response. In the face of any pupil challenge we will vary widely in our reaction, given the different value bases from which we work. While respecting value variation, we do need to offer a high degree of consistency of response to our pupils. Read the following case study and then do the exercise that follows:

' "I insist that she be dealt with in the strictest terms. My standing with the rest of the children depends on it." Mr Allison was livid. Barbara Shaw had told him to "bugger off!" when he told her to go outside at break. The other pupils who had heard the comment had laughed.

'Before leaping into action, the head sent for Barbara, a fifteen-year-old whose inappropriate language had led to previous encounters between them. She was always respectful and contrite on such occasions.

'As usual, she entered his office quietly and waited.

'"Well then Barbara," said the head, "here we are again. And again it's Mr Allison you've been rude to."

'"He was rude to me first," Barbara shot back, unusually hotly.

'"What do you mean?", asked the head.

'"Well, when he told us to get out, he said it to Debbie. And as we were going he said, 'and take your loutish friend with you'. So I said what he said I said to him."'

As usual, things are never straightforward. Is this a story of bad blood between teacher and pupil? Provocation of the teacher by the pupil – or of the pupil by the teacher? Do we have here a head who is insufficiently supportive of his staff? Or is this simply an impossible recidivist pupil who ought to be excluded? Our perception of the case is value filtered, and not infallibly accurate: it will vary from colleague to colleague. The exercise is intended to reduce the rigidity of our reaction, thus enhancing the possibility of collaborative school-policy formulation.

Consider Figure 4.4, a value continuum. Can I invite you to imagine it applies to the vignette above? At one pole is the point that represents 100 per cent support for the teacher, at the other the pole representing 100 per cent support for the pupil.

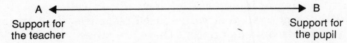

A ←――――――――――――――――――――――――――→ B
Support for   Support for
the teacher   the pupil

Figure 4.4 Response to disruptive incident: value continuum.

It is unlikely (though perfectly acceptable) that anyone will choose a 100 per cent position. What I would like you to do, is, one at a time, to adopt a physical position on the continuum. Then spend one minute completing the statement, 'I place myself here because ...'

This permits a sharing of values that relates directly to pupil behaviour. Occasionally there is some reluctance or embarrassment about starting, but the exercise is worth a great deal of patience. One head of department in a school where we did this exercise said to me that he had learned more about his colleagues in that quarter-hour than in his eight years at the school.

As before, we are not seeking a 'right position'. The activity allows colleagues to pursue collectively the value consensus that the Elton Report sees as a prerequisite of effective school policy-making. It may at this point be opportune to invite the group to produce a consensual statement of values. A number of major companies now produce what they call mission statements – consensual statements of desired ethos. The following, drawn from a multinational corporation, may surprise us but it is adopted by the company because it assists task performance; it provides a lesson for the educator.

That this organization should respect the dignity of all who work here;

That the company ethos should be such that creative risk-taking is not stifled;

That collaboration should be based on consensually derived objectives, rather than coercively imposed directives;

That motivation should be reward based, not sanction based.

Tough values to live up to, but surprising and impressive in the competitive world of business.

Perhaps it seems strange for an educator to end on a note that extols the business world. I do so on the grounds that a shift of perspective can sometimes help us to see old issues in new ways. It is a strategy used by Egan (1982) in helping counselling clients tackle recalcitrant difficulties. This perspective on the world of business has helped me to re-evaluate my position on teaching styles. My early commitment to non-coercive teaching was based on my ethical position that human beings ought to be related to, as far as possible, in non-coercive ways. What I have learned from colleagues in business is that my ethically derived position actually produces the goods in terms of task performance. Collaboration, respect and support alongside challenge are more effective in terms of helping pupils to perform than coercion. A careful clarification of the values that drive my classroom behaviour can be checked against the available evidence on the effect of work climate on performance. As professionals, we can do no less.

CHAPTER 5

Doing it with feeling

The human touch

A young teacher, facing an especially difficult pupil, described his problem to me:

> One girl had been taking things a little too far in previous lessons and had been punished with an essay after a couple of warnings. This lesson she made it clear, right from the start, that she was not going to work and she would do all she could to encourage the others not to work.
>
> When the rest of the class had settled down, she began to chatter and stir up her group of friends. After a couple of verbal warnings, I told the girl to stand in a corner of the room. This was to temporarily remove her from her friends and for the girl *to cool down and feel humiliated.* (My italics)

Here we are in the heart of a disruptive incident, mentally donning our managerial caps and running the various responses through our personal value systems.

The teacher continues, having set his operational objectives of separation and humiliation, to describe the confrontation:

> On this occasion, however, she insisted on shouting to her friends, trying to disrupt the lesson. The next moment she calmly took out a bag of crisps and started to eat them. I recognized the fact that I was being drawn into a direct confrontation in front of the whole class. Losing my patience, somewhat, I ordered the girl to put the crisps in the bin, but she verbally refused, much to the class's delight. Feeling *anger* and *embarrassment*, I bellowed the instruction again, moving towards her. She slowly and *resentfully* put the crisps in the bin.

Oh! by the way, this was a maths lesson. It is important to mention that in passing, because it is a useful reminder to non-teachers of the complexity of the managerial challenge of the classroom. Did the teacher 'win'? I was impressed by his thoughtful, almost painfully honest analysis of an all-too-frequent incident, and would not wish to criticize his moment-to-moment handling of the problem. He brought the incident to the INSET group because he was not happy with the way it progressed. For me, that willingness to self-audit, self-criticize, is the mark of the reflective professional.

It is clear that there is no easy answer, and it is equally clear that the teacher did operate with a personal value base infusing a set of task and social objectives. He wanted order, to defend his personal standing in the eyes of the class, even at the cost of the dignity of his 'opponent', by humiliating her. In this way he could get back to his maths. Yet for some reason he felt uncomfortable with the outcome. In a sense he did win – she did put the crisps in the bin – so why does he not feel like a winner?

The italicized words in the case material are so treated to emphasize the 'feeling'-rich nature of these encounters. Both parties are heavily influenced in their responses by a complicated web of interacting feelings, at the heart of which lies our sense of personal worth. The teacher drops in words like 'humiliate, anger, embarrassment, resentfully' almost peripherally, yet they fuel the movement and pace of the interaction. Alongside management and value issues, feelings, too, need to come under our professional scrutiny.

Spiel's classic (1962) text may provide a clue about why an apparent teacher victory in the classroom can often leave us feeling like losers. He says: 'There is no doubt that by punishment a child can be forced to pay attention. But there is equally no doubt that at the same time, such a child is being accustomed to regard all human relations from the "superior–inferior" angle, and is thus being trained in a basic neurotic attitude. We cannot, therefore, be satisfied with the disappearance of mere symptoms.' The young colleague whose case is recounted above clearly experienced that absence of satisfaction, despite having 'won' the removal of the symptom, the girl's defiance. It is more than likely that this maths teacher was dissatisfied because of the commitment he had, beyond mere control, to education.

In this case, and in many similar incidents, we see two persons collide. There is a battle of wills in which, as Spiel says, the adult can invariably win. Control cannot be our major concern as educators, yet we cannot educate in conditions of anarchy. Our search is for a means of creating a positive learning environment that does not induce in pupils basic 'neurotic attitudes', and for responses to crises that are not based on dehumanizing the pupil. Aronson and Mettee (1965) produced a sobering piece of research. 'When self esteem is damaged, moral controls are lowered', they found. This suggests that for both us and our pupils feelings of being humiliated leave us less likely to use moral criteria to direct or control our behaviour. The classroom can, in such conditions, become an amoral environment. Little wonder, then, that hollow victories based on mutual attempts to crush and humiliate leave us all feeling like losers – exhausted teachers and truculent pupils.

While the response to the kind of challenge delineated above will be personal to each teacher, I would like to suggest two rich veins of knowledge which might be usefully mined. The second, in my view less important, will be explored in detail in the next chapter – the 'What should I do?' mine, concerned largely with the development of skills. For the rest of this chapter I propose to work my way through the caverns of the 'What kind of a person do I need to be?' mine. To put it crudely, we can develop in a soldier great skill in weaponry, but if he is a coward all his skill is useless. What would we do with a surgeon who had the most wonderful medical skills if he always fainted at the sight of blood?

The kind of person I need to be, and all my colleagues must help me in this, is one who has an indestructible sense of personal worth. Although it is now mentioned with greater frequency in teacher education courses, my assertion (McGuiness and Craggs, 1986) that the psychology of the self has had little influence on British pedagogy remains substantially true. It is, still, rarely accorded the centrality of treatment it merits if there is a grain of truth in the assertion of Snygg and Combs (1959) that: 'The establishment, the maintenance and the enhancement of self esteem is the all-inclusive human need, which motivates all behaviour, at all times, in all places.'

A powerful concept, indeed. Awareness of its importance underlies the principle of supportive as opposed to punitive management, and it ought to infuse the practice of our schools, with reference to both our pupils and ourselves. Detailed, scholarly analyses of the concept and its educational application can be found in works by Burns (1979, 1982) and Rogers (1983).

What the research tells us is that we all need to feel a sense of personal worth and dignity if we are to be mentally healthy. When we are deprived of that sense of worth we experience the psychological equivalent of being deprived of oxygen. Imagine your reaction to having a black plastic bag tied over your head. How you would tear at it to regain your access to oxygen – until, that is, you were so damaged that your efforts ceased. So it is with self-esteem: it is essential for our mental health, and we will fight to protect our supply and retain it. So intent can we be on the struggle that all other considerations disappear. As Aronson and Mettee found in their research, even morality goes out of the window. Thus, the able, dedicated, hard-pressed young teacher who figured in the opening vignette could set out, deliberately, to 'humiliate' one of his pupils. Her initial resistance to him, inappropriate as it was in one sense, can be construed as her effort to maintain her sense of worth in the face of this humiliation. Two people face each other, both intent on preserving their self-esteem. They have no choice; if they are mentally healthy, they will at all costs protect that precious commodity.

Our most challenging pupils are often those whose esteem is most fragile. They are wary, suspicious that, yet again, they are about to be demeaned by an adult. Describing work done with severely disturbed adolescent boys, Lennhoff (1965) suggests that 'the symptoms displayed – aggression, withdrawal, school-work difficulties – are nothing else but reactions to the strains and stresses, traumatic experiences, disappointments and frustrations that they have had in earlier life. 'We, the teachers', says Lennhoff, must 'counteract their numerous negative experiences with a great many positive ones.... In our approach to wrongdoing, we try never to plant on a child a feeling of worthlessness.' The expectation is that the misbehaving youngster will learn that *this* adult 'even when she criticises some of his actions, continues unconditionally to accept him'. To ask for this kind of behaviour from the teacher is to ask for professionalism of the highest order, and it begins to tackle the question, 'What kind of person do I need to be?'

It may help to analyse in a little more detail how self-esteem occurs, since knowing something of its structure will allow us to respond more precisely to any danger that threatens it. How can an inadequate adolescent reduce a teacher to barely moral behaviour? What is it about this key human characteristic that makes us so vulnerable when it is attacked?

Fundamentally, our sense of self involves our survival as a person. Severely damaged individuals talk of floating away, of losing contact with themselves, of not knowing who they are. Rogers (1965, 1961) suggests that self-acceptance, without the need to deny or distort parts of one's personality, is a key element in the development of a healthy self. Having a clear, accepted sense of self is crucial to my mental health, because it involves my very existence in a fundamental way.

The absence of threat to my sense of self allows me to develop a healthy self-esteem. I am able to respect myself, and that is the springboard which lets me reach out respectfully to others. The person who lacks a sense of respect for self finds it impossible to give respect to others. So where does this self-esteem come from? We can see in Figure 5.1 a simplified representation of its structure.

We all carry around in our heads two mental constructs. The first is a *self-image*, which is a product of the response of my environment to my behaviour. Thus I perceive myself as athletic, good-looking, intelligent, witty and kind, because the response of my family, friends and acquaintances to my behaviour has been to give me prizes when I run, flirt with me when I dress up, ask my advice when they have a problem, invite me to give after-dinner speeches, and say 'how kind' on numerous occasions. There is, of course, more subtle feedback, and not all my self-perceptions are positive. They also vary from one environment to another. But basically, we all carry around with us this self-image, which is fed into us from our environment.

The second construct is an *ideal self* – that is, my perception of the characteristics that are valued in my social milieu, whether this is the family, the club or my place of work. I am able to internalise a composite of the valued person in this environment. There may be variation from one environment to another (e.g. for an adolescent, the peer group and the school), so we cannot rely on cross-environmental consistency.

Given the two constructs, we compare them for congruence. In a specific environment, the greater the match between my perception of self and my view of the valued characteristics in that environment, the greater my degree of self-esteem. There will be a strong tendency to frequent places and people where my self-esteem will be enhanced – and to avoid or resist possible reductions in my level of esteem. We can and do try to manipulate either of the two constructs – witness the six-year-old who is slow to start reading. Self-image: I cannot read. Ideal self: Readers

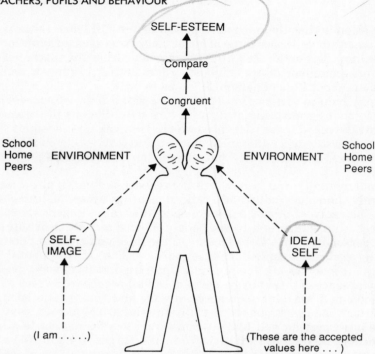

Figure 5.1 Achieving self-esteem, the 'all-inclusive human need'.

are valued here (home/school). No match, diminished self-esteem, but esteem essential. I have heard such a child say, 'Reading's daft, girls do it. I don't like it.' He is trying to distort the ideal self.

The important thing is that self-esteem is an *essential* correlate of mental health. It is in that sense that Spiel can write of punitive class-room management as 'training children in basically neurotic attitudes'. It eats into the most precious thing the child has – his or her self. This is not to condone ill-discipline or loutish behaviour; it is to ask questions about our objectives and strategies. The result of strategies which fail to use the constructs outlined above was described by McGuiness (1983): 'These children are invited day after day, for fifteen thousand hours, to contemplate their worthlessness in terms of what their teachers and schools evidently prize most highly.' There can be a chasm between the self-image given by school to the pupil, and the ideal self presented. Self-esteem, essential for mental health, becomes an impossibility, and the pupil either accepts the training in neuroticism identified by Spiel, or fights back with disruption. McGuiness continues, 'Those pupils who learn the lesson of docility, must carry away from school an indelible impression of their inadequacy and inferiority. Others, who have more resilient attachment to their sense of personal worth, reject school as an inauthentic commentator on their personal worth, by truancy or disruption – these we label deviant.' I need to label them in this way to protect my own self-esteem as a professional. The disruptive pupil threatens my sense of worth as a teacher, and I can fall into the 'all lose' response where pupil and teacher try to destroy each other. The psychology of disruptive behaviour suggests a high 'pathogenic potential' in simplistic responses to complex problems.

The entitlement of the pupil seems to be quite clear. The most recalcitrant of our charges has the right to a respecting, esteem-enhancing environment, in which careful management of the pupil's experience in the classroom will ensure optimum balance between the level of challenge and the level of support. The teacher must offer a planned productive tension between the risk latent in the learning experience and the safety of the learning group. This is not as complex as it may sound; as teachers or parents we will all have observed that young people will respond to the most difficult challenges, *when they trust the challenger*. To phrase it in the language used earlier, pupils accept the invitation to learn when the teacher displays highly developed social leadership skills. We do not need to surrender our self-esteem to be an effective social leader – indeed the contrary is the case.

Teachers are human, too. It would be foolish to suggest that our duty to our pupils should contain an element of self-destruction. We too have a right to a respecting environment, as Mary asserted in the case discussed in Chapter 3. The difference between our right and that of the pupils is that, as the professionals, we have responsibility for both our own and the pupil's self-esteem. It is when the two come into apparent conflict that we can be tempted to protect *our* self-esteem by assaulting the child's. However, as we saw at the beginning of this chapter, the ritualized humiliation of the pupil does nothing for the self-esteem of the teacher. Later in his letter this teacher describes himself as 'feeling a sense of admitting defeat'. I was struck on reading the letter by how similar that phrase was to one used by a nurse on a course analysing reaction to patient death. There was the same feeling of being de-skilled, rendered useless, incompetent, and the same tendency to shoulder a level of responsibility of messianic proportions. The response, too, to this inappropriate shouldering of responsibility was similar: stress, a mild feeling of depression, feeling down. We need to take responsibility only for *our* actions. We cannot carry the burden when our pupils choose to be less than human, any more than the nurse can be responsible for the death of a patient. But responsible for *our* actions, we are.

The answer to the paradoxical demand of simultaneously caring for myself and my pupils lies in the answer to the question, 'Who am I?' Lack of self-respect makes it more likely that I will demean pupils, and the greater my own sense of personal worth, the greater my ability to respond to the most challenging pupils. We need to work very hard at our own sense of personal worth.

Tackling the question, 'Who am I?' should be a central part of the professional development of teachers at all stages of their careers, but it is a tough question, and for that reason is often avoided. The challenge posed by the question can considerably exceed the level of support within the group where it should be raised. Yet if we do not tackle it, we will go through our professional lives extending enormous amounts of psychological energy maintaining a façade. That is exhausting work, which leads inexorably to the stress and depression mentioned above. Less exhausting in reality, though possibly daunting in prospect, are the following exercises, designed to facilitate supported self-exploration and esteem-enhancement, with their pay-off of increased teaching effectiveness and lower stress. Do I really have respect for myself during my contacts with pupils?

On an initial teacher education course in Durham, having been asked to identify any personal traits or characteristics, any element which might reduce their effectiveness as teachers, the students, as we all could, produced long, honest lists. The most interesting thing for me on this occasion was a comment of one student, when the exercise was finished. She said that she was completing the last of four years of preparation to become a teacher, and that this was the first occasion, in all that time, when she had been asked to look specifically at herself. She had examined child psychology, curricular issues, materials, the skills of teaching – but at no time had she been asked to consider, 'Who is this *me* that I take into the classroom and present to my pupils?' Yet, as she eloquently put it, 'I must be a key factor in the classroom equation.' A key factor, indeed, and well worth the most nurturing development.

It is no coincidence that Elton's 'recommendation 42' is that 'Initial teacher training establishments should introduce all their students to basic counselling skills and their value', and equally no coincidence that the first training exercise in Egan's (1986) influential counsellor training manual is the one described in the previous paragraph: 'What personal traits or characteristics reduce my effectiveness as a communicator?' Counsellors must, says Egan, 'come to terms with the problematic in themselves'. No less can be expected of teachers.

The activities suggested below explore the significance of the self, both in preventing and in responding to pupil disruption. It may feel comfortable at one level to 'professionalize' our response, to use a façade to keep our pupils at bay. The reality is, however, that everyone engaged in the 'game' is at least subconsciously aware of it, and, however hard we try, the real 'me' will always affect the interactions. In Figure 5.2 we can see the complexity of the exchange.

The effect of the real 'me' in the area of pupil behaviour cannot be sidestepped. We make a major analytical mistake if we think that the teacher 'in role' can somehow pass through the managerial task of setting objectives, using skills and techniques to implement those objectives, without any intervention or influence from the self. My experience in this area has consistently been that difficulties involving pupil behaviour most often involve 'self' issues – problems arise or deteriorate because of some element of the self of the teacher. This is in no way to try to attribute blame; it is simply to state that, whoever was to blame, a greater degree of comfort with self would have improved the outcome. Skill (to be looked at in detail in the next chapter) needs to be developed on that secure personal base.

The activities follow the structure of development of self-esteem by exploring first the image we have of ourselves in the professional context,

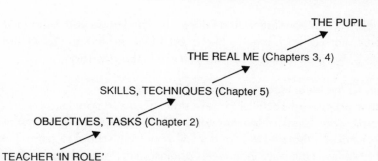

Figure 5.2 Mediating influences between teacher and pupil (based on an analysis in Gilliland and McGuiness, 1989).

then the perception we have of 'the ideal teacher', with reference to pupil behaviour, and finally the implications of these two constructs for our self-esteem.

A summarizing exercise will examine how our sense of personal worth might flow into the classroom and influence our teaching.

Activity 1: my self-image (approx. 15 minutes)

Return to the exercise in Chapter 3: 'Teaching that harms — or helps' (p. 23). Using the list of positive and negative characteristics in teachers, identify your teaching style in relation to each trait identified by ticking either the 'just like me' (1) or 'not at all like me' (2) box. If you have not yet done the earlier exercise, either do it now or use the following collation of results from recent INSET courses:

HELPFUL TEACHERS	(1)	(2)	HARMFUL TEACHERS	(1)	(2)
are warm, accepting	☑	☐	bully	☐	☑
inspire, enthuse	☑	☐	are sarcastic, put you down	☐	☑
care, talk to you	☑	☐	humiliate	☐	☑
encourage, are patient	☑	☐	make you feel guilty	☐	☑
listen to you	☑	☐	are insensitive	☐	☑
respect your ideas	☑	☐	demean you	☐	☑
give you time	☑	☐	make you feel in the way	☐	☑
really love their subject	☑	☐	seem bored by the subject	☐	☑
like questions	☑	☐	seem defensive	☐	☑
make you feel good	☑	☐	are bossy	☐	☑
smile, have a sense of humour	☑	☐	push, hit, shout	☐	☑
are themselves, real	☑	☐	pretend all the time	☐	☑

Add any other qualities you see as significant.

Briefly discuss your lists with a colleague who knows you, sharing your perceptions of each other — be honest, but positive. You should end up with a sharpened image of who you are in the classroom.

Activity 2: the ideal teacher (approx. 15 minutes)

What process of socializing new staff in your school occurs? In other words, what 'ideal' of teacher competence is projected to newcomers to the school? Whatever it is (and it will vary from school to school), that is what staff will measure themselves against, in their search for professional self-esteem. It may be useful, as a diagnostic tool, to use a distinction elaborated by Best *et al.* (1980) between the rhetoric and the reality of the concept. Are we saying things that a subtle, hidden agenda subverts? In pairs, produce a list for general sharing with the whole group, of items you would suggest as: 'the qualities my school values in its teaching staff'. Be as specific as you can. Produce the list under two heads:

The Rhetoric   The Reality

Briefly discuss both lists, considering particularly the implications for practice of any split between rhetoric and reality.

Activity 3: feeling good as a teacher (approx. 15 minutes)

The research suggests that to remain mentally healthy we need to be able to perceive a congruence between the way we see ourselves and the key values of our working environment, i.e. between our self-image and our ideal self. If that is not possible, we can either alter our self-image in the direction of the ideal (INSET goals), review and alter the ideal that our organization is presenting to its members, or lapse into stressed self-undervaluing.

Analyse with your partner the extent to which any of these three options is occurring. Each of you should answer the following questions:

- Do I feel able to value myself as a professional in my current circumstances?

- What do I need to do to maintain and enhance (or establish?) a high degree of self-esteem (about me, about my organization)?

If we do not value ourselves, the challenge of valuing difficult children is almost insurmountable.

TEACHER REACTIONS TO THE EXERCISES

These activities are very challenging, and will be more successful the more supportive the learning environment. Self-esteem is such a central requirement that we can only really examine it when we feel truly risk free. The group leader needs to combine a sensitive, supportive, gently humorous atmosphere for the activities to be productive.

Typically, teachers are very honest, identifying their good and bad points. There is some tendency to pre-emptive self-criticism, which colleagues should be encouraged to correct – 'What do you mean, you bully? I've heard that you were really helpful to Billy Adamson when his Gran died.'

It is useful to end this very taxing session on a high and positive note. Each group member can be asked to produce an empty 'booklet' by stapling together sheets of paper equal in number to the people in the group. They will put their name on the top sheet (Figure 5.3). The book-

Figure 5.3 Learning to give and receive compliments.

lets are then filled in, page by page, by each member of the group, who for each colleague will complete the sentence, 'One thing I have valued from you during this session is …'. The entries can be anonymous, and it should be stressed that this is a valuing exercise, designed to set self-esteem high on the agenda. Just this once humour, banter, kidding ought to give way to careful reflection and open, supportive communication.

It seems to be surprisingly hard to give or receive compliments – almost embarrassing – yet such positive input helps all of us bloom, pupils and teachers alike. Working with a group of teachers I was fascinated to observe two solid PE chaps almost writhe with embarrassment at the suggested exercise. I hoped desperately that they would not use humour in a deflective, defensive way, and I explained the importance of the supportive nature of the exercise. When we had completed it most of the group read their 'booklet' with great attention. Their two colleagues, to me sadly, thrust the messages from their colleagues deep into their pockets, unread. You can imagine my delight, as I drove home after the session, to pass them both parked at the side of the road, clearly reading the documents in the privacy of the car. I hoped, and am sure it was the case, that they would continue their journey, esteem enhanced.

Of course the division between the self and our skills is artificial. I have emphasized it here because the importance of the self is so regularly sidestepped. Having highlighted it, we can now pass on to the analysis of a number of key skills in responding to disruption.

CHAPTER 6

Red alert!

Responding to crisis

The classroom nightmare exercise, suggested as an ice-breaker in Chapter 3, invariably throws up the kinds of incident that set the alarm bells of all of us jangling – the refusal to obey, the crude, public, racial insult or sexually harassing behaviour, the apparent breakdown of order in the whole class. My argument so far has been that all of these horrors become less likely if we engage in a confident, managerially competent, respecting dialogue with our pupils. Such classroom behaviour requires highly professional skills of the teacher. However, even when such abilities are sensitively deployed, we do and always will come across the critical incident, its origin a mystery to us, its continuation a threat and a source of profound anxiety. Classroom crises do occur, and we need to develop a range of effective strategies to respond to them. Can you relive this teacher's experience?

A rather violent incident occurred in my classroom after (1) morning break. The class was a (2) third-year English group which consisted entirely of (3) boys as the girls were in the hall viewing (4) a sex education film. I had been teaching this particular class for about (5) six weeks, and although they had been (6) a bit rowdy, I had had no cause to reprimand any of them seriously.

While waiting for the girls (7) to return, we had begun to compile a crossword, and most of the boys seemed to be interested, and proceeded to work. Suddenly (8) two boys began fighting and I quickly realized that it was for real. From the (9) other side of the room, I rather (10) disdainfully told them to sit down – one of the boys did, reluctantly. The other remained defiant, folding his arms, and standing. I asked him if he was going to (11) deliberately disobey me, and he replied, 'Aye.' I began to move towards him, in what I knew was a vain attempt (12) to intimidate him. He showed no sign of submission and refused to move. I told him to get out and to my dismay he again refused and dared me to make him. I approached him and realized he was preparing to hit me (13). There was total silence in the class.

The incident is one shared by a young teacher on an INSET course, with an implicit question, 'What on earth do I do?' It is a critical incident, a time of 'red alert'. The bracketed numbers in the account identify some of the significant data. In terms of INSET, the micro-analysis of such material is an invaluable opportunity to take a measured look at things that normally happen so fast that our reactions are automatic. What we need is some kind of analytical tool to make sense of the foregoing, and a clear, extensive repertoire of behaviour to respond to it. The elaboration of these two elements is the major task of this chapter.

(1) Are there any danger points in my day? Times: after break, after some specific class, before lunch, etc. Classes: are some groups more taxing, some pupils more demanding, does my rhythm take such variations into account or am I a one-pace performer? Subjects: is my French trouble free and my German a disaster area? An ability to analyse in this detailed way is a great help to problem-solving; as a manager you need full data.

(2) What do I know/need to know about thirteen- to fourteen-year-old male adolescents? Can I/should I treat them the same as year one pupils? Do I advert to age variation in my planning of lessons? What is my value-governed response to gender issues?

(3)(4) Here is a class which would normally be mixed, but which is currently segregated for sex education. What messages are being given to pupils here? Will I find that my teaching is about to be strongly influenced by a context not of my making? Is there a staff forum in which such topics can be openly discussed?

(5) Only six weeks' contact – little time so far for establishing mutually respecting relationships. Can I find strategies for achieving mutual respect more quickly?

(6) Have I been clear in establishing acceptable codes of conduct in my class, or have I been too weak in accepting a woolly compromise?

(7) Is this lesson seen by me, or by the pupils, as a time-filler while the girls have their sex education? Task leadership skills, in such a situation, require the teacher to present both groups with well-planned, well-presented material. If the pupils think there is one law for the rich and one for the poor, the poor will throw up their own alternative tasks and their own alternative task leaders.

(8) 'Suddenly' – things can happen out of the blue, but a meticulous observation of each pupil in the class can often give us some degree of early warning. The unobtrusive but all-seeing eye can be developed by all teachers.

(9) The teacher is clearly distant from the action. Physical mobility, presence can give the teacher the atmosphere in different parts of the room. The 'desk hugger' is ceding territory in a potentially explosive way to the class.

(10) 'Disdainfully' is a strange word to use – 'looking upon someone with contempt or scorn', says the dictionary. Is that the managerial strategy of the teacher? Given research on self-esteem, what kind of a reaction can be expected?

(11)(12) The confrontation is established. Another all-lose situation has been set up, with a real possibility of violence against the teacher. (13)

Fortunately, this incident ended without violence, when the teacher backed away and sent another pupil to bring the deputy head. A 'victory' was won, leaving the teacher 'so panic-stricken that it took me hours to pull myself together'. 'Afterwards,' he said, 'I always felt extremely embarrassed in front of that class.'

Could the incident have been tackled differently? There is always an almost infinite number of ways of responding, none of them 'correct' (different values, objectives, individuals, talents, moods), but some of them more effective and satisfying than others. No one could feel happy at being panic-stricken. Aside from the crucial, broad issues of managerial styles, values, personal confidence and feelings of self-worth, which we have already examined in some detail, we can and should carefully examine a number of specific skills available to us in encounters such as the one described above. They are based on investigations carried out by social psychologists (Argyle, 1988; Trower *et al.*, 1978) into the way individuals function in group contexts, and though the psychologists were not looking specifically at education, the findings have proved useful in our attempts to help individual teachers and pupils to function more effectively in the group context of the classroom.

Groups are both supportive and threatening to the individual: we are drawn to membership, yet constantly feel the group's potential to overwhelm our individuality (Thompson and Kahn, 1970). Many people experience this in the family – a tension between the security of belonging and the fear of being somehow stripped of individual significance. The group leader's task (the task of parents in the family, teachers in the classroom) is to maximize the support and comfort in belonging without threatening the sense of self of the individual members of the group. We seem to have been here before, with a different group of theorists, in Chapter 3 – the management specialists and the balance of support and challenge; the development of tasks *and* social leadership skills. The impressive contribution of Argyle and his colleagues is that they explore the mechanics of how it's done.

My own functioning in a group needs to be put under a microscope. Here I am, a teacher of modern languages, with a degree that says I have a modest competence in that area, but no indication that I can lead a group, the context of 99 per cent of my teaching. The first activity at the end of this chapter will offer the group a microscope under which to place its interaction.

A second set of activities explores in practical terms the findings of Argyle, with special reference to the importance of non-verbal behaviour.

Argyle's research offers the classroom practitioner (or any professional involved in interpersonal work) a precise tool for examining the nuts and bolts of group leadership. Basing his findings on hundreds of hours of detailed observation, Argyle offers two very helpful insights: human beings are much more influenced by non-verbal than by verbal communications; and non-verbal communication can be broken down into a manageable group of categories for diagnostic and analytical purposes. Given this finding, we clearly need to look carefully at our non-verbal communicating.

Argyle does not argue that our verbal interactions are not important. He presents powerful evidence to suggest that if there is a contradiction between our verbal and non-verbal inputs, the message listened to will be the non-verbal one. I am reminded of an article I once read that discussed, in all seriousness, 'The use of the phrase "sit down" as a means of eliciting standing up behaviour in children' (the source is lost in the mists of time). Frequently we verbalize ideas that are in total conflict with our body language. We say, 'No, I'm not angry', 'I'm fine, thanks', 'I will not start this lesson until I have complete silence' – while our more truthful bodies say, without words but more powerfully, 'I'm furious', 'I feel awful', 'Just lower the sound to a level where I can shout myself hoarse over the top of you'.

Obviously the potential for disruption, not to say chaos, in such an environment is enormous. Using non-verbal skills, understanding what messages others in the group are sending, and trying to establish congruence between my verbal and non-verbal communication must be priorities for the reflective practitioner.

Argyle observed that individuals present to each other in groups messages about their interactive intent – my immediate intentions in this group at this moment. The people in a classroom, a staffroom, at a party or a conference communicate to each other a range of messages about intended styles of relating. There is a subtle, constant negotiating of position, as each individual seeks the comfort of support or the stimulus of challenge, the warmth of safety or the bracing breeze of risk. Whether the embrace of the group is reassuring or stifling is a question of balance, just as an element of risk can be paralysing to some and stimulating to others. How do we send these messages to each other?

The research identifies seven 'roots of social behaviour' – a battery of potential behaviours open to all of us. Argyle is not identifying 'personality types', he is asserting that, as humans, we have at our disposal a range of behaviours that allow us to engage in very subtle interactions with other people in our group. Some of us, for whatever reason, limit our choice to a smaller number of items in the repertoire, but this is our choice, not a statement of some personality deficit. It is not that there exists a type of human who *is* unassertive; there are some humans who have not developed the skills in this area. But if they want to, they can.

In a group, of whatever kind, I will convey to my fellow group members my intentions on the following roots of social behaviour:

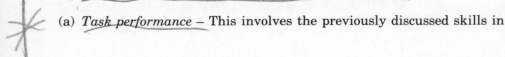

(a) *Task performance* – This involves the previously discussed skills in task leadership. What are we *doing* here? How can we do this most effectively? Let's not waste time.

(b) *Dependency* – We signal to the rest of the group our willingness to be led, to take a subordinate role. This communication can be used to gain help and guidance, but it can also signal an unintended abdication of responsibility.

(c) *Affiliation* – This communication emphasizes a commitment to social contact, safety and comfort in the group. It involves the previously discussed skills of social leadership.

(d) *Dominance* – Here, the group member signals clearly an intention to direct, take control, organize: a key skill for the teacher.

(e) *Sexuality* – The sexuality of a group cannot be ignored as it is an important influence on its functioning, and not just in the sense of female/male attraction. Classrooms (and other groups) are full of dynamics involving male/male attraction, female/female attraction, male/male competition and female/female competition. Such factors can powerfully influence group functioning.

(f) *Aggression* – Communicating the need or desire to strike out at others in the group. As we have seen, there are some severely maladjusted children, who may respond aggressively towards perceived sources of threat; and indeed anyone whose self-esteem is under attack may respond aggressively.

(g) *Self-esteem* – This refers to the kinds of messages sent to establish one's sense of worth in the group. Any group that crushes such messages inevitably provokes the crushed person into defensive action: this can be aggressive and destructive of the group, which is perceived as a destroyer of the individual.

So there it is. All our group activity involves an interchange of messages about the seven roots of social behaviour. We can play individual notes on this interactive scale, subtle harmonies of two or three notes, majestic arpeggios – and we do so with words and actions.

This is the broad overview. We must look, too, at the detail of the messages sent. How do we detect that pupil X is being, or is about to be, aggressive? How can I communicate my task intentions *and* also send out messages of affiliation? Can I restructure an aggressive message from a pupil into an affiliative one? (One experienced teacher was slightly jostled by a hulk of a lad in the school-yard. 'Out of the way, granny!' he cried, in hot pursuit of the ball. 'Tom!' she replied coolly, 'do we presume that was meant as a compliment?' 'Oh, yes Miss, sorry,' he said, and was off again. She had beautifully reconstructed a potentially unpleasant incident by receiving what could have been aggression as affiliation.)

The words we use are usually quite clear: 'Come on, we must finish this by break' (Task); 'OK, Mary, can you take us through what you've discovered so far' (Dependence); 'Does everyone feel happy, so far?' (Affiliation); 'Right, that's enough. I want you all to listen carefully, and if necessary take notes, and I'll run you through the procedures' (Dominance); 'I really like your new hairstyle/That style makes you look like a pimp, tart' (Sexual); 'I can guarantee that when you open that big mouth of yours, an idiocy is going to come out' (Aggression); 'I just wanted to say that I've enjoyed working with you all on this project. It's been super' (Self-esteem). The problems are often created when we are simultaneously sending out contradictory non-verbal messages. As mentioned earlier, the research is quite clear that in such conflicting situations, attention is paid primarily to the non-verbal message. Practitioner folk-lore tells the tale of the wise pupil reputed to have told a teacher, 'What you are speaks so loudly that I cannot hear what you say.'

Argyle identifies a number of non-verbal communicators that run alongside the words we say, either reinforcing them or undermining them. It is these elements that we can deploy to operate more effectively in the challenging classroom, so that instead of unconsciously sending out conflicting information about our intentions in the group to pupils, we can become much more congruent in combining the verbal and non-verbal. In research carried out in Durham with young teachers, we often found a high level of incongruence between spoken and non-verbal messages. We need to become expert in exploring the potential and impact of our non-verbal behaviour.

Body contact is a powerful communicator. How could it be otherwise, given that it is our first method of communicating with others – the skin to skin of baby and mother? Much fascinating work by social psychologists leaves no doubt of the enormous influence of this non-verbal message. Of course, as teachers we are a little wary of being dubbed a 'touchy-feely'. Recent revelations about sexual abuse have left us sadly reluctant to touch – in stark contrast to our neighbours across the Channel. The reluctance, of course, is a fear that the touch be misconstrued as a sexual touch. But touch, and all non-verbal interpersonal skills, are not specific to any one type of behaviour. Thus, touch can be aggressive (hitting, poking an accusatory finger into the chest of a pupil), dependent ('George, give me a hand while I get down this ladder'), affiliative (ruffling hair, shaking hands), and so on. The key thing is not that we constantly go around school touching people but that we realize that touch is a powerful, complex, multi-significant communication – available for use when we decide it is appropriate and comfortable.

Promixity refers to the messages sent out in a group by the degree of physical closeness of the members. Am I a teacher who clings to my desk, ceding large tracts of the classroom to 'pupil control' like some self-imposed no-go area? Or do I use proximity to signal that I take responsibility for *all* of this territory – no 'rebel-dominated' strongholds in my class. Pupils send out their own non-verbal messages to their teacher. I have observed them skilfully arranging their desks to make themselves inaccessible to the teacher – a strong non-verbal dominant statement to the teacher from the pupils. Some teachers realize the need to 'get in among them', but cause disruption and confrontation by unreflective use of non-verbal behaviour. Dominant response to dominant pupil behav-

iour results in exhausting confrontation; the young teachers on our
course soon developed much more subtle approaches that combined a
dominant touch and proximity with warm verbal behaviour. Their entry
into the 'no-go' area (dominant) occurred while teaching continued: 'so at
this juncture, the Boers decided ...'. As the breaking up of the close-
packed desks took place there was a series of brief affiliative inputs: 'Can
I just squeeze through here?' Desks shift at the courteous, unobtrusive
request. 'Thanks ... Do you mind Tim ... that's fine. You were packed in
like a Boer defensive ring, there.' Then the teacher remains to teach from
the newly 'taken' territory, establishing clear control. No confrontation,
merely a subtle combination of dominant (I'm in charge) and affiliative
(you won't be crushed by me) messages. It is impossible to offer a package
using this type of material; what teachers can do is to develop awareness
of the impact of the full range of non-verbal behaviour, learn to read it
early in pupils and respond to it by drawing from a full personal repertoire of non-verbal skills.

Posture also speaks to our pupils. Can we learn something by reflecting on
the posture of Margaret Thatcher, John Major, Neil Kinnock or Tony
Benn? Can we become critical observers of the non-verbal as well as the
verbal communication to which we are exposed? We are not seeking the
perfect posture – it doesn't exist. We *are* seeking to divine the effect of our
own posture on those with whom we work, and reflecting consciously on
the impact the posture of others has on our response to them.

Our *gestures* add extra meaning to what we say. Have I ever looked at
them? Do I stab the air with an admonitory forefinger, administer karate
chops to it, caress it with cupped hands? Does it matter, make a difference? We can only answer that by practising, observing, reflecting and
learning.

And what of our *eye-contact*? One modern linguist whom I watched
wrestle with a taxing class never established eye contact with any pupil.
She would yell, 'I want complete silence' (dominant) while staring unre-
mittingly at a point on the back wall (dependent). The pupils accepted her
more powerful, non-verbal communication. As with all the other modes
discussed, this can be used to bolster messages on any of the roots of social
behaviour – dominant eyes, dependent eyes, aggressive eyes and so on.
With the linguist, I asked her, in the safety of the INSET session, to
choose a colleague she felt comfortable with, and to practise 'holding gaze'
– to look into each other's eyes for as long as possible. She declared herself
incapable of that, but gradually built up from a furtive, fearful nano-
second glance at her companion's face, to a solid, brave, three-second
holding of gaze: a small addition to the range of skills she was taking into
the classroom. Back in school she tested out her skill, looking, quite
deliberately, at each child as she gave her lesson: dominant eye contact,
saying 'I see all, know everyone here – there is no anonymity in my
classroom.'

In contrast, a very able physics teacher we worked with reported difficulty with one class, a third-year group. Watching him teach, it seemed
that his highly developed dominant behaviour was leading to some self-

protective resistance from the group. He lacked an affiliative input, the ability to say both, 'I'm in charge here' and 'You're safe with me in charge'. Unlike the teacher described above, this one had a gaze that would bore holes in sheet steel. We practised a range of affiliative behaviours in a closed-circuit television studio in the university, and the outcome was delightful. It was reported in McGuiness and Craggs (1986: 27):

> During a lesson on states of matter with his 'problem' group, a couple of girls crowded round his demonstration bench and began to misbehave. He stopped, looked fiercely, fixedly, unsmiling for a few seconds and asked in a firm voice, 'how many ice-cubes did you have in your dish?' 'Three sir,' came the rather cowed reply to his dominant behaviour. The look continued momentarily, and then melted into a hint of a wink and a smile as he said, 'OK, just checking you're keeping up with me.'

His skilful switch from strong task and dominant messages to affiliative communicating was almost certainly unconscious, but the fruit of much practice in the TV studio. The purpose of this practice was not to establish some kind of patterned behaviour for the teacher, but to offer the opportunity to raise awareness of and explore one's own range of interpersonal skills. Classroom management is inevitably idiosyncratic: each of us must manage out of our own repertoire of talents. It is a repertoire that is often underused.

We can also put under our microscope *head movement, facial expression* (have I forgotten that my lips can turn up at the corners?), *physical appearance, grooming, voice tone, modulation* and *volume.* The search is still not for an ideal: our task is to develop an awareness of the impact of non-verbal messages on people with whom we work.

It is frequently the case on INSET courses that once the idea of using non-verbal behaviours in a more conscious, knowledgeable way is established teachers all want to work on the skills of dominant non-verbal communication – using proximity, touch, orientation, posture, voice quality and so on to say, 'I am in charge here.' I hope that the extensive discussions on safety, social leadership and self-esteem will have indicated that there is more to the effective management of a group than the ability to dominate. Argyle makes it clear that purely dominant behaviour can have the counterproductive effect of driving the dominated to some form of self-protective behaviour. To keep a control lid on any group will lead to outbursts of assertions of independence. We have all come across the teacher with (probably unexamined) high skills in dominance, and had the misfortune of picking up his or her class afterwards. The pupils are bursting to break loose from the control, and I'm left with the option of continuing the high-dominance style of relating or trying to combine control and care. If I, and the whole school, opt for the lid-on policy, the pupils charge out of school at the end of the day 'free' and eager to express that freedom, sometimes in anti-social ways. If I try to work more reflectively with dominance *and* affiliation, I will initially reap the inevitable harvest of inconsistency. The effective teacher, as we have already seen, must protect the sense of safety in the group by guaranteeing the self-esteem of its members as a basis on which the learning tasks can be pursued – in Argyle's terms, dominant and affiliative messages must be communicated together. An example can illustrate this, and indicate that the theory underpinning the approach is not limited to teaching.

I was slightly disturbed to note, as I sat in my local, that two very drunk, quite large young men were beginning to make a nuisance of themselves. The landlord discreetly phoned the police, and two very young officers arrived. By this time the drunks were standing behind the quizmaster of an inter-pub competition, calling out the answers and ruining the game. They thought this was hilarious. I was intrigued to find out how the police officers would handle the trouble (and glanced around for a quick exit in case a fight broke out!). Having spoken briefly to the landlord, one policeman approached the pair and addressed the rowdier, more belligerent of the two:

'Excuse me [politely, Affiliative], sir [Dependent], I'm afraid the landlord would like you to leave' (Task). The policeman stood tall in his helmet (Dominant), and close to the delinquent (Dominant). The verbal message was conciliatory, respectful and polite – the much more powerful non-verbal message was unequivocally dominant. Had the words been dominant, too ('OK Sunny Jim, *out!*'), we could well have had a fight.

The drunk took a couple of steps back (unconsciously trying to reduce the dominant position of the officer): 'Why, we're just havin' a bit of fun, man.'

'I know that, sir' (Affiliative), said the officer, taking a couple of steps forward (maintaining Dominance). 'But I'm afraid the landlord is absolutely within his rights in asking you to leave.' Two more steps back to reduce the dominance were skilfully restructured by the policeman as acquiescence to the request to leave. 'Thank you, sir,' he said, as he held the door open, and the pair departed. It all happened very quickly, and it was only later that I was able to analyse the incident in this way. The young officer, I'm sure, had had some training in combining dominance and affiliative *behaviours* as the most effective way to establish a dominant *relationship*.

It is clear that the skilful verbal and non-verbal communication of the behaviours related to the roots of social behaviour can be deployed preemptively as well as in response to crisis, but let us concentrate on the 'red alert' aspect of the scenario with which the chapter opened. The crisis could perhaps have been pre-empted, but it wasn't, and it needs to be tackled. The fight has started. Can I find anything helpful in the work of Argyle that will help me to respond effectively? You will recall that the teacher 'rather disdainfully told them to sit down'. Intention clear – to defuse the crisis.

How could we analyse that initial message? The teacher suggests that he gave a dominant verbal message, 'sit down', with a dominant (or even aggressive) non-verbal overlay of contempt and scorn: a contrast with the policeman's more complex communication. In Argyle's analysis of interaction, a dominant or aggressive 'self-protective' response is very likely, and it came. In no time, there was a highly visible stand-off, with both parties suddenly finding themselves desperately protecting self-esteem. We'll return to that in a moment, but let's check on alternatives to the highly dominant approach adopted. Remember that the non-verbal message is more influential, so we will probably find that this should contain the dominant message. But it should be neatly designed to keep the pupil (respectfully!) on the hop, by arriving wrapped in some affiliative verbal input. Each of us will use Argyle in a personal way, so the following is an example, not a programme for action!

'Brian, Tom! [use names to personalize, remove anonymity, give respect – not, as I have heard, 'You, girl', 'Hey, you, lad'], you've got a whole break to faff around in.' (This reconstructs the violent behaviour into something less serious – faff – giving them both an out, and a cooling-down period.) While setting a clear, not a threatening, verbal tone I can walk with relaxed posture, facial expression, etc. right up to them, thus giving my powerful non-verbal, dominant statement. Then 'Come on, lads [verbally affiliative], settle yourselves down until break and then let your hair down.'

It is important in exploring responses to emphasize and re-emphasize that we are not engaged in a search for the perfect response – we are broadening our response repertoire, increasing our room for manoeuvre. It is very useful to bear in mind, too, what many good teachers do intuitively – that contrasting of the verbal input (e.g. dependent, affiliative) with the non-verbal (task, dominant via proximity, orientation, touch, eye contact, etc.), which is very effective in establishing a dominant relationship. This is not to say that on occasions we will not need, and want, to hammer home an unequivocal dominance by sending out dominant messages, both verbally and non-verbally. The point is that we make *aware* decisions on the issue – *that* is professional, and the following exercises are designed to increase that awareness.

Activity 1: people in groups (approx. 20 minutes)

Invite the participants to assemble in groups of not less than eight, and not more than twelve. Tell them that they are to be given ten minutes to arrive at a consensual statement defining 'school ethos'. In itself, the task is valuable, but for the purpose of the exercise the real area of interest is the dynamic of the group as it sets about its task. If the facility is available, it is salutary to video the proceedings. After ten minutes, briefly share the group statements, then ask the group to spend the remaining time discussing the following:

- Did one person take charge of the group, as soon as the task was given?

- How did that occur? Why him or her? (Task leadership, dominance, aggression)

- How did the 'followers' feel about this leader? (dependence, affiliation) Did anyone say little, or nothing? What blocked them?

- Did anyone want to contribute, but fail to? Why?
- How did that feel?
- Did the group note anyone's concern for, or skill in, creating a safe climate?
- Was any group member skilled in involving the less assertive group members?
- Would the group see itself as tending towards task or affiliative behaviours?

The subsequent general discussion can examine the implications of the group's functioning for classroom interaction.

Activity Two: beyond words (approx. 30 minutes)
This exercise invites colleagues to explore their range of comfort with and awareness of different non-verbal communicators. Given their power and their priority over verbal messages, an opportunity to do some *practical* analysis seems appropriate.

Body contact (Only do those things which feel comfortable)
In pairs: Shake hands with your partner. How does it feel? Be as perceptive and open as you can. Now shake hands again, and pat your partner's right shoulder with your left hand as you do so. Is it different? In what way?

In threes: Decide who is to be A, B and C. A will be an observer. B takes one hand of C in both of his or her hands, and gently strokes it. Change over roles. How does it feel? Are you comfortable — as toucher, touched.

In pairs: Can one partner sit on the floor and extend a hand to be helped to his or her feet by the partner? Change roles. Discuss how it feels to give/receive dependent touch.

In pairs: Take it in turns to lift your partner off the ground. An actual lift is not essential — take up the position to do so. How does dominant touch feel?

Discuss touch/contact with special reference to affiliation, dependence, dominance. Bear in mind the enormous power of this non-verbal communicator; do not lightly set it on one side, or under-scrutinize it.

Proximity
In pairs: Stand facing each other at opposite ends of the room, and walk slowly towards each other, until the proximity is no longer comfortable. Do you both stop at the same time? Is one person's discomfort initiated by the partner stopping?

Full group: Sit in a way that resembles that of a class. In turns allow each group member to address the 'class', from behind a desk, in front of the desk and in the middle of the class. Discuss how the different positions generate different messages — from the point of view of both 'class' and 'teacher'.

Orientation

In pairs: Concentrate hard on the different response evoked by having a partner talk with you from the following positions:

you on a chair, your partner sitting on the floor;

both on chairs side by side;

both on chairs face to face;

your partner standing in front of you; behind you.

Discuss how each of the orientations feels. Begin to analyse the intensifying effect of combining all three — e.g. standing, close, behind, with hands on the shoulders of someone (dominant) or squatting, alongside, holding one hand in both of yours (affiliative). Keep in mind that non-verbal messages can be garbled, just as verbal ones can. Stay open, analytic, experimental and reflective.

Eye contact

In pairs: Hold gaze with your partner for a count of ten, or as long as feels comfortable. Try the same exercise, infusing the look with anger, affection, concern, flirtation — you are allowed to laugh!

Non-verbal communication merits careful analysis. Most teachers use it constantly, but without reflection. It is a bit like letting words pour out without any evaluation.

Activity 3: getting it together (time varies according to number in group)

Invite each group member to prepare a brief presentation for colleagues (5 minutes maximum). It is important to invite each individual to analyse his or her own tape, looking particularly at the non-verbal dimensions of the presentation — the foregoing and the following: *posture, gesture, head movement, facial expression, physical appearance, grooming, voice peripherals.*

Each participant can be invited to produce a personal audit of social/ task leadership skills, of ability to communicate dominance and affiliation, and a diagnostic statement of areas for development. Figure 6.1 gives an example of an analytical schedule used by the Durham project in collaboration with a group of teachers.

VERBAL INPUT	Very task oriented – no praise
VOICE volume	Good – nice variation from whole class to
tone	individual. Occasionally 'strained' if
other	reprimanding
PROXIMITY	Too desk-bound. Distanced relations!
ORIENTATION	Stands all the time – formal feel
TOUCH	None
EYE CONTACT	Very dominant; hawk-like
POSTURE	One hand on hip (seems aggressive)
GESTURE	A stabber – one finger
FACIAL EXPRESSION	Unsmiling, but not aggressive
GROOMING	Very smart – formal (contrasts pupils)
PHYSICAL APPEARANCE	Physically tall, heavy

Figure 6.1 The dynamics of the classroom.

TEACHER RESPONSES TO THE EXERCISES

It is useful and reassuring to remind colleagues that detailed attention to non-verbal impact is not some weird innovation dragged in from a Californian commune! Such training is commonplace in all professions which have an interpersonal dimension. It is, nevertheless, challenging to subject ourselves to this degree of scrutiny, and it can only be done productively in an atmosphere of real trust. When colleagues express reservations about, for example, stroking the hand of a fellow teacher, it is important not to push, but to respect and *use* the reluctance. How frequently do I ask pupils to engage in tasks that threaten them in some way?

Teachers will typically press for an answer to the question – 'OK. We've done all the things you suggest, but the pupil is *still* there, defiant, offensive, potentially aggressive. What do I do next?' They are quite properly posing a 'worst-case' scenario, and it is important to explore it. My initial reaction is some pleasure at the 'I' in the question – not, 'what would *you* do next?' It allows us to go where the competent manager must go first, to objectives. What, precisely, does the teacher want to achieve in this situation? The issue of priority is high on the agenda. Let's reset the scene. In the original incident, the teacher left to seek help from a senior colleague. We can change the ending to one where the confrontation remains in all its frightening ugliness: the pupil squares up to the teacher, verbally and non-verbally signalling aggressive intent. We presented one case study on film to colleagues, in which the teacher tried to take the arm of a pupil (dominant), saying, 'Come on you. Out.' The pupil, very aggressively, shook off the teacher's hand with an equally fierce, 'Gerroff! F*****g gerroff me.' Now what?

One clear option is to continue with the physical attempt to eject the pupil. The advantage would be a clear dominant message to the whole class that the teacher is in charge and his or her word is law. The strategy has obvious attractions, but it runs the risk of pushing the teacher into the 'neurosis inducing' approach rejected by Spiel (1962), discussed in Chapter 5. There is also a real possibility that the pupil may be physically stronger than the teacher, more desperate and consequently more out of control, or that one of the parties in the physical confrontation will be injured. Of course, all teachers have the same right to self-defence against aggression as any citizen, but this presumes that the pupil has initiated an attack. Here that has not occurred. Is my objective here a more subtle one? Not simply to control, but also to educate in an atmosphere of mutual respect (cf. Chapter 4). Would not the pursuit of such an atmosphere require me to play close attention to the esteem-enhancing nature of the encounter? Here, I think, lies a key element in the management of the critical incident – how can I maintain my self-esteem in this situation without accepting the confrontational, physical challenge of the pupil? My position as a teacher would lead me to seek that kind of a solution – I have a distaste for aggression, and regard any need to resort to it as a (sometimes inevitable) last resort, a confession of educational failure, which I would concede with the utmost reluctance. I do not see myself at that point in this situation yet.

If pre-emptive measures have failed to head off the problem, persuasion has not diffused it, and I have set on one side the initiation of a physical confrontation, I seem to be accepting that my limited options will lead me to seek to:

defuse the tense situation;

establish clearly that the pupil behaviour is unacceptable and *will* be dealt with at a more opportune moment;

psychologically separate the malefactor from peers;

leave myself feeling 'in control' of the situation (esteem intact);

leave the pupil with some rag of esteem, to cloak a withdrawal on his or her part;

Return to a task-rich, dominant-affiliative class with minimum disruption.

A tall order, indeed! But then, most professional orders are demanding. Chalk-face teachers are brilliant at creative response to the above types of objectives; collectively, over several courses, they have suggested the following:

At the first 'Gerroff! F*****g gerroff me!', immediately remove your hand (dependent), but associate that with an affiliative 'Tom', and a dominant, standard setting. 'We all [affiliative inclusion of whole class] know that that behaviour is totally unacceptable, and you and I will need to sort that out later. The rest of us have a lot of work to do. So, settle yourself and you and I can take our time to discuss this with [the deputy head, parents] at break time. I'm sure you understand that you've gone past an important boundary, but I can't waste any more of the class's time. We'll discuss it at break. [Note use of 'I', 'we', 'you', 'The rest of the class', to establish mental sets of allies and opposition.] OK. Can I apologize to the rest of you for that waste of our time? Let's see if we can make up what we've lost.' Again, this is not presented as a model but as an extender of possibility. It may not pacify Tom, but it does give us a new slant, a different approach from the confrontational. The detail, the verbalizing, the non-verbal behaviour will vary from individual to individual.

The key to developing this much more flexible response repertoire is self-critical practice on case material with colleagues. The Appendix contains a number of case studies for such attention. It is important to *operationalize* the responses even in discussion – not to say, 'I would tell him to sit down', but to act it out. In that way, we begin to feel the difference between, 'Sit yourself down, lad', and taking a chair, placing it next to the chair of the pupil, sitting down yourself, and saying, 'Let's sit down and discuss this like adults.' No programmes, no panaceas, but a real alternative to knee-jerk, confrontational responses to pupil challenge; and all the time having the skills in dominance to deploy if it becomes necessary to declare, 'The buck stops here.'

CHAPTER 7

Fire!

Launching a school policy

Teachers are not saints, nor are they superheroes, nor can we expect them to be. Their job is demanding and too much is expected from too few resources. Schools are failing not because of a lack of will or a lack of caring on the part of the school staff but because they labour within an archaic, inefficient and inhospitable organisational structure and set of social demands. (Schostak, 1983, p. 221)

As I suggested in Chapter 2, we need to bear in mind that we do not work in a vacuum. Our professional activity takes place in a strongly influential school ethos and the larger environment of our society. This contextual element must be borne in mind by all involved in the education of children, if we are not to make inappropriate morale-sapping demands of teachers.

The Elton Report makes 138 major recommendations on the subjects of teachers, schools, parents, pupils, attendance, police, governors, LEAs and central government. Some of the issues are subdivided into discrete elements, and it is possible to derive a school policy checklist of items for the attention of a school working party (governors, parents, teachers, pupils). In the opening chapter it was suggested that generating the right questions was more difficult than coming up with the right answers. The recommendations of the Elton Report, framed as questions for 'my' school, direct our attention to the heart of effective policy-making on pupil behaviour. The temptation to select or simplify what is a complex and lengthy list could lead us to omit just the element which requires attention in school A or school B. Somewhat reluctantly because of the uncongenial length of the list, but very deliberately given its centrality in formulating school policy, the following issues from the Report are presented. As a minimum, a school should have detailed data on the following:

- What training in classroom management skills has been made available to staff members? (Recommendation 1)

- What opportunities have staff had to analyse or discuss work on personal qualities as teachers? (R2)
- What special attention is given to new teachers and the process of induction and pupil behaviour? (R7)
- Do governors take 'full account' of the personal qualities of applicants in making appointments? (R8)
- Is the headteacher trained in personnel management 'in the broadest sense', and in the management of change? (R14)
- What is the quality of communication – within school (teachers, pupils), with parents, governors, the community and outside agencies? Evidence? (R15)
- How would you describe the sense of community within the school, its ethos and its relationship with its host community? (R16, R17)
- Does the head lead on pupil behaviour; consult and seek consensus; monitor it regularly? (R17)
- Is there a visible, operating system of managerial support (referral procedures, back-up, case conferences) and of peer support (safe, respecting groups)? (R19)
- Are decisions on pupil behaviour monitored for their effect on teacher and pupil morale? (R20)
- Are such decisions clear, consistent, based on principles, with a declared, *healthy* balance between punishment and reward? (R23)
- Are they also characterized by fairness, consistency, flexibility, with a clear distinction between major and minor infractions? (R23, R24, R25)
- Can you be sure that no group punishment or humiliating punishments occur? (R24, R27)
- Is a serious effort made to detect at the earliest opportunity any bullying or racial harassment? How? (R28)
- Are victims supported and protected in the long term? Does the school have an ethos where such attacks are reported by pupils easily? (R28, R29)
- Are the behavioural implications of curricular decisions fully monitored (material, teaching methods, pupil grouping)? (R30, R32)
- Are school resources equitably distributed; are *all* pupils able to have a frequent experience of success, reward? (R33)
- Is the potential of PSE and the pastoral care system maximized in developing positive pupil behaviour? (R36, R37)
- Are there clear aims for the use of the tutorial period, a rich opportunity for developing pupil responsibility? (R38)
- Is there a *systematic* collection of pupil views on school behaviour, and is use made of those views? (R39)

- How would you describe the relationship you have as a school with outside agencies/support services? (R40)
- What trained counsellor presence do you have on the staff? All new staff and *at least* senior pastoral staff should be trained in basic counselling (R43)
- Is there a clear 'care of premises' policy which ensures a clean and attractive working environment for all? (R44)
- Is the school regularly decorated with the work of students, as a way of enhancing pride in the common facilities? (R46)
- In constructing the timetable is due attention given to the behavioural implications of times, movement and class–teacher match? (R51)
- Are *senior* staff regularly visible at strategic points during the mass circulation of pupils? (R52)
- Are pupils allowed access to the building outside lesson times? (R53)
- Is there a clear, planned policy on behaviour over the lunch break, with training for non-teaching staff involved? (R54, R55, R56)
- Are parents involved in their children's social as well as academic development at the earliest possible opportunity? Are they written to in appropriate language, made welcome in school? (R57–R61)
- Could a course be offered to parents to help the pursuit of recommendations to parents? (R68–R74)
- Are pupils involved by the use of records of achievement, compacts, or other means in taking more responsibility for themselves and their progress? (R75)
- Do pupil records include information about their pastoral needs as well as their academic needs? (R80)
- Has the school explored the potential benefits of 'support teams' as an alternative to premature exclusion? (R86)
- Does the school have a declared, monitored policy on the issues of gender and culture differences? Are staff trained in the skills needed to respond appropriately (e.g. in responding effectively to non-verbal or verbal behaviour which comes from pupils of a different cultural background to their own)? (R89–R93)
- Does the school have a clear policy and practice on truancy? Has liaison and consultation taken place with education welfare officers, police and other involved agencies? Are random checks carried out by senior staff on individual lessons? Are the governors fully involved in policy-making and informed regularly on outcomes in practice? (R99–R100, R101, R108)

It would seem to be appropriate for professional development days to take account of these issues, and the example in the Appendix of a possible programme has been designed to create opportunities for them to be analysed and operationalized. I have recently found the practice of evening INSET, with parents invited, to be very productive, and a governor presence seems to me to be essential.

Important though it is to establish the database described above (see Figure 7.1 for an overview), the key to effective school policy-making on pupil behaviour lies in what we *do* with that data. Action will vary according to the different context within which schools work, but there is a consistent batch of 'areas for attention' which seems to concern most schools.

GOVERNORS:	Full, updated information, involvement in policy-making
HEAD:	Ethos creation, leadership, personnel skills, management
SENIOR STAFF:	Support, consistency, high visibility, counselling skills
TEACHING STAFF:	Opportunity for personal development, skill training
PUPILS:	Protected (from bullying, racism, sexism, appropriate curriculum). Involved (systematic collection and use of pupil views)
PARENTS:	Regular consultation
CURRICULUM:	Appropriate, fair resource distribution, use of tutorial period, pastoral care and PSE to enhance pupil responsibility
SANCTIONS:	No group punishments, no humiliating punishments
REWARDS:	All pupils have access to rewards/success, praise levels high

Figure 7.1 Overview of key issues from the Elton recommendations.

ETHOS

Eaton (1979), in analysing factors associated with pupil absence, found that school was a stronger influence than home. This was not an isolated piece of research, but part of an increasingly persuasive pattern that highlights the great importance of the school for the social, emotional and behavioural development of children. Power *et al.* (1967), Reynolds (1976) and Rutter *et al.* (1979) established a clear relationship between what Rutter referred to as the 'ethos' of the school and the behaviour of pupils. In analysing the variation in outcome across a number of London schools, Rutter *et al.*'s detailed statistical conclusions allowed them to say that the differences were 'not due to such physical factors as the size of the school, the age of the building or the space available; nor were they due to broad differences in administrative status or organisation'. This study did find, however, that they 'were systematically related to their [the schools] characteristics as social institutions'. The general conclusion was that 'schools can do much to foster good behaviour and attainment and that even in a disadvantaged area schools can be a force for good'.

There is no research support for a fatalistic view that we can do little to respond effectively to difficult pupils. On the contrary, there is a powerful and growing body of evidence that by altering the insensitive, demeaning, rejecting, failure-rich experience of many pupils, and striving to establish a respecting, valuing and non-threatening environment, the behaviour of pupils can be improved dramatically (Grunsell, 1980; Bird *et al.*, 1980; Galloway *et al.*, 1982; Schostak, 1983; Vaughan, 1983; Steed *et al.*, 1983; Tattum, 1986).

The most detailed attempt to get inside the mechanics of 'ethos creation' remains the work done by Rutter *et al.* In establishing a school policy, the analysis of Rutter *et al.* suggests that we ought to examine a number of influential issues:

Group management
- Task management skills (well-prepared lessons, materials and apparatus ready, punctuality, smooth transitions).

- Style of discipline – relating style ('Frequent disciplinary interventions were linked to more disruptive behaviour in the classroom. Conversely pupil behaviour was much better when teachers used an ample amount of praise.')

- Ability to spot trouble early, and respond non-dramatically.

- Awareness that an intended disciplinary intervention may become an unintended reward to attention-seeking, thus sustaining the undesirable behaviour (cf. the use of the phrase 'sit down' as a means of eliciting standing-up behaviour in children).

- Awareness that stopping the misbehaviour of one child may be interrupting the work of others.

- Awareness that the negative atmosphere created by constant nagging can provoke or perpetuate disruption – this is not to say that the reprimand is inappropriate, rather that it *can* aggravate the situation instead of improving it.

Expectations and standards
- Labelling theory indicates clearly that those publicly and consistently designated deviant will begin to live down to the label. Equally, clear expectations of success and socially appropriate behaviour lead pupils to behave in the expected way.

Teachers as models
- Rutter cites evidence that pupils use teacher behaviour as a model for their own behaviour. The considerate and respecting teacher will draw such behaviour from pupils. The violent, aggressive, bitter teacher will be used as a model by pupils, too.

Feedback

- There are some surprising findings on the usefulness of prizes and punishment in the research of Rutter. It seems that since formal prizes go to only a few pupils, the others have lowered motivation as a result of the discouragement experienced. The *proportion* of pupil awards should be high if we are to achieve a positive effect. Rutter is unambiguous – while he advocates a balance between rewards and punishment, he says 'praise, rewards and encouragement need to outweigh negative sanctions'. Heath (1977) found that schools with formal punishment systems had worse pupil behaviour.

Consistency

- Pupil behaviour is better in those schools where there is a consensual approach to behaviour that seeks to develop a system that responds to the legitimate needs of the whole school community.

Relationships

- Staff willingness to share pupil concerns, listen and talk to them about matters other than academic ones has a positive effect on pupil behaviour. Rutter also draws attention to the usefulness of shared activities as a means of establishing greater cohesiveness between teachers and pupils – he accepts that this suggestion is based on other research than his own: 'One of the consistent findings from other research is that shared activities towards a common goal which requires people to work together are a most effective means of reducing inter-group conflict.'

Pupil responsibility

- Rutter's research shows that a high proportion of pupils benefit from being involved in positions of responsibility in school. Improved academic performance was another feature of those schools who involved pupils in decision-making.

The findings are very complex, and Rutter and co-workers emphasize the cumulative and interactive nature of the effects. Nevertheless, it is clear that a grid for examining a school's ethos can be produced, and the audit carried out either by the school itself or by an outside consultant.

Beyond ethos lies a range of more concrete elements. I recently spent several instructive weeks with colleagues in a secondary school who, having analysed their hoped-for and actual ethos, decided that the next most influential element was the school curriculum, its content and its mode of delivery.

CURRICULUM

Rutter's finding that 'appropriate academic emphasis' correlated positively with good behaviour suggests that it, too, is an area which merits some attention. Rutter accepts that the concept itself is difficult to pin down, and was unable to draw a clear inference from his data about what constituted appropriate academic emphasis. McGuiness (1989), using research on the effect of level of self-esteem on motivation, suggested a checklist for heads of pastoral care, which may offer some insight into this area of influence on pupil behaviour. Some of the parallels with the list of recommendations in the Elton Report are clear.

Are academic and behavioural aims of the school planned in an integrated way? Do the staff check, estimate the likely consequences on pupil behaviour of academic decisions?

Is the school's examination policy developed with the needs of *all* pupils in mind, whatever their ability? Is project work for GCSE fair in the sense that the strong support some children receive from home in terms of micro-computing facilities in statistics courses, extra book resources, parental expertise and so on, is counterbalanced by a school-based resource for pupils not similarly advantaged?

Does the school signal clearly to the school community that all pupils are valued, regardless of academic skill?

Can prizes be won by a large proportion of the pupils, from all groups in the school?

Is pupil work publicly valued by display, publication or presentation to a wider audience?

Is strong attention given to 'matching' curricular material to pupil ability? Is a serious attempt made to ensure that able pupils are stretched and less able pupils given appropriate material?

Are teaching methods of *all* staff regularly monitored? Is this done in a safe way, so that teachers see such monitoring as part of a professionally appropriate stance? Are social leadership skills in the classroom given the same status as task leadership skills?

Does the school make its policy on the grouping of children with due regard for the effects of such policy on behaviour? Is this monitored? Are data available on the academic, social and emotional effects of streaming, setting, banding and mixed-ability grouping?

Is homework seen by pupils as punitive? Is there a clear school policy on the purpose of such work? Do those children who have to do homework in crowded, television-dominated surroundings receive additional support and understanding from school? Are parents involved in policy-making on this specifically collaborative aspect of their children's education?

Is it possible for all pupils to 'establish, maintain and enhance their self-esteem' in the academic climate of the school?

Such a careful study of the effect on behaviour of the academic activity of the school does no more than the available research demands – it checks the interactive results of the skills in task leadership and social leadership of the staff. Yet, given even the most competent curricular offering, some pupils will still resist their teachers' attempts to enthuse, motivate, engage or teach them. They are a small proportion of the pupil body, but they do need a special response. The colleagues from the comprehensive school mentioned earlier, having scrutinized their 'ethos' and put their curriculum under a very professional microscope, established that they still had about 10 per cent of the pupils who represented a serious challenge to their ability to create a positive learning environment in the school. This particular school decided to develop four main responses at whole-school level to the challenge of their most difficult pupils.

The *case conference* was seen as offering several special advantages in teachers' efforts to deal with their most difficult pupils. All staff were invited to identify, with a brief explanation, the pupils whom they found most difficult. Interestingly, the expected overlap from teacher to teacher did occur, but it was paralleled by the appearance of a number of subject- or teacher-specific disruptives. Several younger teachers expressed relief that they now knew they were not alone in finding 'Davey' or 'Helen' a handful, or were delighted to discover that a team response to a special problem was to be generated, and carefully monitored at the case conferences that followed. 'You don't have that awful feeling of being on your own in hostile territory,' one probationary historian said to me.

The structuring of the response constitutes the meat of the discussion, and decisions vary greatly from school to school. It may prove beneficial to establish small teams of staff with responsibility for challenging pupils. The teams (using the techniques of team teaching) will comprise at least one senior, skilled teacher, whose job is not only to coordinate the response to the pupil, but also to develop the professional skills of new colleagues. The discussion of the specific needs of a pupil can usefully go beyond the team formed at the case conference to the pupil himself and his parents, with a clear documentation of the problem being tackled (truancy, bullying, insolence, failure to submit homework on time, etc.), the proposed plan of response, with the agreement of the pupil and the support of the parent documented as a form of 'contract' between all concerned. Vague verbal exchanges tend to float away after a few days, whereas a written statement of intent intensifies the commitment to change and is a helpful record of any progress.

In discussing *contracting* as one aspect of the initial counselling encounter, Nelson-Jones (1982) describes a technique which can help in working with particularly challenging pupils. It is aimed at 'arriving at a working model, and the formulation of working goals and methods'. Where Nelson-Jones uses the words 'counsellor and client', I have substituted the words 'teacher and pupil'. He sees the process as involving the teacher and pupil in arriving at a 'formal or relatively formal agreement concerning treatment goals and methods'. He sees it as important that the teachers offer a summary statement that is clear and checked by the pupil for accuracy and adequate coverage of concerns. The nature, level and amount of material in the summary need, he says, to be tailored to the needs of the specific pupil. The following paraphrases an example offered by Nelson-Jones to counsellors (1982: 283):

'As I see it, and I've had long discussion with all of your teachers

before our chat, the main areas of difficulty seem to be ... How do you
see it? Am I being unfair, have I missed out some important bits? OK,
perhaps the time has come to draw it all together and talk about
where we go from here. Do you have any ideas about the next steps?
... Right, what your teachers would like is ... Can you give that a go?
How do your Mum and Dad feel about that?

'What I'll do now is get this written up so that we all have a clear
record of what we've all said and agreed on – and it will give us all
something clear to aim at.'

Nelson-Jones emphasizes that the presentation needs to be clear, free of
jargon, and designed to enlist the pupil's motivation. It is not a punitive
encounter; it is a collaborate pursuit of part of the pupil's education, and
it must be monitored and evaluated with the same rigour as any other of
the teacher's professional interventions.

A third technique identified by the school in question was *behaviour
modification,* that slightly mysterious, vaguely disconcerting approach to
difficult behaviour that most of my generation saw vividly in its aversive
form in the film, *A Clockwork Orange.* The very power of the techniques
of behaviour modification is part of the explanation of our unease with it.
There seems to be something 'inhuman' about it. It can appear to be
distant from the ideals of the educator, more in tune with the skills of the
animal-trainer: it is redolent of rats, pigeons and dogs! Despite all that,
my colleagues in the school mentioned decided that, after careful attention had been paid to ethos and the curriculum and individual contracts
had been established with a small band of very difficult pupils, there
remained in that band an even smaller group who seemed to be incapable
of fulfilling the contract. They displayed such a high level of inconsequen-
tial, unpredictable and uncontrolled behaviour that, even in small
numbers, they had profound negative effects on the learning of the other
pupils in their group. In our INSET discussions behaviour modification
programmes for individual pupils were identified as the next step. Krumboltz and Thoresen (1976), Axelrod (1977) and Eaton (1979) offer a clear
path through the ethical and technical challenges of using behaviour
modification. Krumboltz and Thoresen assert that 'the criterion for
success in any educational endeavour is changes in behaviour on the part
of our clientele', thus challenging us to declare objectives clearly and
monitor levels of success in attaining those objectives. Sutton cites extensive research which establishes the high success rates of behavioural
approaches with the most difficult subjects, and Axelrod offers a set of
procedures and examples specifically for the use of teachers.

McGuiness summarizes the major findings, identifying five major
points for consideration by staff (1989: 114–16):

Definition: It is essential that the behaviour to be modified is defined
precisely. To speak of 'disruptive outbursts' or 'persistent naughtiness' is
inadequate as a base for action. They are evaluative comments, not definitive statements about actual behaviour. 'Shouting out in class',
"swearing', 'punching other pupils', 'refusing to sit at his desk' are precise
statements that allow us to formulate precise responses – to initially

reduce and finally eradicate John's shouting, or swearing, or punching, or refusal to sit.

Environmental Influence: Another aspect of the database we need to produce a plan for action is the 'social' perspective. Where does the specific misbehaviour occur, in what circumstances (teacher, room, subject, following or preceding which activity, in what kind of weather, in what particular domestic environment). We will usually discover that apparent 'constant' misbehaviour is occurring in very clearly definable situations.

Classroom Based: The response needs to be clearly based in the classroom. The programme designated will take into account the baseline established in the two earlier points.

The Programme: We need to ask what reward is sustaining the undesirable behaviour. Behavioural psychology offers the teacher the principle that people behave as they do because that behaviour gives them pleasure. We need to discover what pay-off John gets from his shouting, swearing, punching or standing up. We can use John's own view here, not in a disparaging or threatening way, but to involve him, as far as possible, in managing his own behaviour. Does he enjoy the peer approval, the attention, the purple face of the apoplectic teacher, the obvious fear he can engender in the teacher, a feeling of power? In using behaviour modification, the insights of the client are a key source for analysing the database, the environmental element and the issue of reward.

It is important not only to remove the pay-off for the undesirable behaviour, but also to reward any move towards the desired behaviour. It is unrealistic to expect dramatic, immediate changes; we need to guide the pupil forward by rewarding a series of increasingly acceptable 'successive approximations' to the desired behaviour. Given a clear data baseline, we can discuss and reward improvement as well as total success. Clear records and regular discussion with the pupil are essential for this to occur. Axelrod (1977) is quite clear on this: 'In order to modify student behaviour, teachers will have to modify some of their own behaviours. They will have to keep daily records of their students' performance. They will have to be systematic. They must be willing to fail and try again.'

What to the teacher may be perceived as a reward, may be received by the pupil as an excruciating punishment! Some pupils hate public compliments, but really appreciate the quiet word of congratulation. If we want to extinguish the good behaviour in the pupil who hates public acclaim, all we need to do is to congratulate her publicly! To work out an acceptable reward, it can be very fruitful simply to ask. I would share with the pupil a simple explanation of the theory we are to use: 'George, we've talked a lot about the way you've been messing up other people's working time, and your own, and we have our contract. Can I suggest a way that might help you stick to the contract? People can do the hardest things if they get some reward, however little, for doing them. I was trying to think what you would like as your little reward. I'm not sure whether you would really want me to say anything about how well you're doing in front of the whole class. Let's say you really reduce your swearing, would you like to be able to...?'

The rather technical matter of 'schedules of reinforcement' (the effect on behaviour of rewarding at different rates) indicates that behaviour established by constant reward (e.g. receiving a small present each time you visit a petrol station) disappears very quickly when the reward is stopped. Behaviour that receives intermittent reward on a fixed ratio (e.g. on every fourth occasion you receive a wineglass at the petrol station) persists longer. Most persistent is behaviour that is intermittently reinforced on a variable, unpredictable ratio (as with a one-armed bandit). Unfortunately, aside from the positive use that can be made of this finding, we sometimes discover that one teacher's sterling effort to remove the reward for a pupil's misbehaviour is subverted by another teacher's unintentional variable rewarding of the behaviour.

The case conference is an important forum in which to guard against this. The peer group may also have to be involved if they are not to act as rewarders of the behaviour. The other pupils can, with the target pupil's permission, be brought into the contract: 'Let's see if we can help George to ...'. Evaluation: Regular, shared evaluations of the declared objectives by the pupil and the teacher offer reinforcement for both.

The use of behaviour modification in the ordinary school is most helpful with the small group of very challenging pupils. It is time-consuming, but there is ample evidence of its power in the most discouraging circumstances. The staff of the School Psychological Service are very helpful as consultants in the use of this technique.

I have left *counselling* to the end because it infuses all the ideals in this book. The Elton recommendations to offer training in counselling skills have already been mentioned, but we still find in the world of education an ambivalent attitude towards it. McGuiness (1989) quotes an astonishing DES (1987) document, which described counselling as 'having big ears and nodding at the right time'. It is astonishing in the ignorance it displays of the nature of counselling, and in its patronizing dismissal of an activity which stands close to some of the most demanding challenges of our time: responding to the needs of the sexually or physically abused child, helping the bereaved person cope with loss, working with the many victims of disaster on post-trauma stress. It also seems to be unaware of the wide range of commercial and business concerns that offer training in the skills of counselling to their senior staff in the knowledge that this will enhance organizational performance. Groups who have sought work on counselling skills in the recent past include industrial and commercial managers, general practitioners, nurses, careers officers, police officers, the armed services – and increasingly teachers. It should not have been necessary for Elton to have to recommend training in counselling skills; the current demands that are made on schools (both staff and pupils) led one business colleague to express amazement at the absence of 'human resource' support in them. As the large corporations develop staff expertise in the area of counselling, we see a parallel decline in the number of counsellors available to pupils in our schools, and staff are left shamefully undersupported through the most dramatic and demanding changes the education service has seen. Two journalists, Heller and Judd, recently (1991) cited research carried out at Manchester University Institute of

Science and Technology, which concluded that 'there is too much change, introduced too quickly and poorly managed'. All this with minimal personnel help for staff and pupils. A disruptive response seems inevitable.

Could counselling skills help? It seems that quite a few hard-nosed commercial organizations think so, given the investment they make in such training. What they expect to gain is the benefit of their staff learning to offer a 'relationship whose characteristics create for the client an environment of such safety, respect and support that he finds it possible to take the risks involved in independence and a creative response to life's challenges' (McGuiness, 1989). We find ourselves completing the circle begun in Chapter 3: managers must make it possible for their staff (and in our case our pupils) to take creative risks, to be independent, taking responsibility for themselves.

There is no such thing as snap training in counselling, despite the attempts by some organizations to suggest otherwise. The minimum number of hours required for the most basic certificate is 100, and both the British Psychological Society and the British Association for Counselling are producing criteria for personal or course accreditation which are vastly more time-consuming than that. The teaching profession needs to have personnel trained to those high standards. Nevertheless, the 'basic skills' recommended by Elton can be developed in less stringent conditions. Many of the exercises in this book are concerned with personal awareness, autonomy, responsibility and the skills of relating – it is impossible to lack these skills and to teach well. How dispiriting, then, to find O'Hear discussing teaching and teacher training from his powerful position as a member of the Council for the Accreditation of Teacher Education, and displaying the same ignorance about the nature of teaching and the same patronizing dismissal of an activity that stands close to some of the most demanding challenges of our time, as that displayed by the (now withdrawn) DES document cited above.

Rogers (1983) makes the connection between counselling and effective teaching most clear in his book, *Freedom to Learn for the Eighties*. He argues powerfully that the facilitating relationship of counselling, with its talent-liberating potential in personal life, presents the same possibility of personal development in the classroom. At the heart of Rogers's position is the consistent finding of researchers that successful outcomes in the kind of learning that counsellors' clients do correlates not with this or that technique, but with a clearly identifiable kind of relationship. Rogers (1962, 1965), Truax and Carkhuff (1967), Carkhuff and Berenson (1977), Brammer and Shostrum (1982) are at one in claiming that the key to becoming a more effective individual is the presence of a number of core conditions in the teacher–learner relationship.

The first is the infusion of the relationship with *unconditional positive regard*; that is, the message that both people in the relationship are possessed of inviolable dignity. As a teacher, I am more effective if I can let my pupils sense that this attitude pervades my relationship with them. It is not an abdication of responsibility or dilution of standards of behaviour; it is the creation of a haven of security for even the most resistant and objectionable pupil. Care for the esteem of both parties is essential if the encounter is not to deteriorate into the no-win confrontations discussed earlier. As a teacher I need to be able to share with the pupil a warmth and commitment to help, a willingness to understand that clearly declares that I value the pupil as a person.

The second condition is the presence of *empathy* in the relationship; that is, a willingness to go to where the pupil really is and accept the reality of his or her perspective. It involves the demanding skill of being able to listen non-judgementally, so that defensive silence is changed into collaborative sharing. In a real sense I have to learn to see the world through the eyes of my pupils, while remaining able to maintain the authenticity of my own perspective and being able to communicate it in a non-threatening way. It involves the ability to be where the pupil is without becoming enmeshed in the often rigid perceptions that have brought the pupil into the relationship in the first place. It needs a willingness to be *genuine* in the relationship (the third core condition), not a façade meeting a façade, or two players in a game. The challenge to me here is to be honest and open, not exploitative and manipulative. It feels hard to put the three together – and the heart of counsellor training involves an experiential exploration of this challenge.

We cannot, as professionals, set that challenge on one side. The weight of the evidence from research and practice in other professions is too strong to allow us to sidestep it. Interpersonal work at all levels produces more effective outcomes when it is characterized by the core conditions.

So, as I promised at the outset, I have offered no recipes. I hope that the foregoing has opened a larder stocked with the best ingredients, and am happy to leave the individual confections to the professionalism and creativity of school-based colleagues.

CHAPTER 8

Growing as professionals
Words into action

The last ten years or so have been years of enormous change and stress for the teaching profession. It is time to consolidate, review and evaluate the impact of the changes. From Callaghan's famous Ruskin speech (1976) to the present we have been invited to focus on tasks and subjects; the 1960s' identification of the importance of the climate within which tasks and subjects are pursued has been discounted. Yet the emphasis on subject competence (and attendant SATs), so heartily promoted in the National Curriculum, can blind us to the strikingly obvious fact that mastery of a subject is a necessary but not a sufficient condition for successful teaching. Perhaps the great failing of the National Curriculum (undoubtedly it has also contributed positively to our vision of the purpose and potential of schools) is the absence of any real awareness that there exists a complex range of inter- and intra-personal issues that crucially affect whether or not children actually learn those carefully constructed subjects and tasks.

It is not a coincidence that as NCC/SEAC-driven professional development courses on the academic and its assessment abound, teachers (with the financial support of their schools) flock to courses on counselling, tutorial work, classroom management skills and the broader issues of teaching and learning. As professionals and practitioners, they know that young people will not learn unless they as a profession can master the complex skills of motivation. It is sad that the flailing (yet politically influential) attacks by Lawlor (1990) on the teacher education programmes of several British universities seemed to be made without awareness of the fact that the focus of her wrath (i.e. a reflective, theory-informed monitoring of practice) is an approach currently being *bought* from those same schools of education by industrial and commercial concerns. It is ironic that hard-headed business concerns pay commercial rates for courses that Lawlor so airily dismisses. The business community sees clearly what she is ignorant of: that the quality of task performance is enhanced or diminished by the ability of the manager to motivate. So it is with teaching. Pupil learning can be enhanced or diminished by the skill of the teacher as a motivator. An 'in at the deep end' approach to management would be regarded as folly of a high order, yet the Preface to Lawlor's pamphlet argues that 'The skills of teaching are essentially practical ones – they can be acquired only through experience, trial and error and careful individual supervision.' As a parent I would urge our political masters not to subject my own or anyone else's children to 'trainees' learning by trial and error. As a profession we must resist attempts to turn us into a group of uncritical replicators of someone else's (Lawlor's?) vision of education.

In that uncompromisingly professional spirit, this section will describe an exploratory, non-prescriptive course outline for colleagues. INSET providers and tutors involved in initial teacher education will, of course, select those issues, elements and exercises which seem appropriate to the group being worked with, and the following structure in no way seeks to remove flexibility. In the same way, the Appendix of further case material is offered merely as an additional resource to course planners.

SAMPLE COURSE: WHOSE CLASSROOM IS IT ANYWAY?

This is an example of a twelve-hour/two-day course, which can be re-formed to meet the time or target group required in a specific situation.

Rationale: Whatever the route taken by the teacher in the profession, the costs of training that teacher makes it important that we do not lose expensively trained personnel because of avoidable deficiencies in classroom management skills.

There is a growing body of evidence that many teachers are surviving in the classroom by using strategies that are damaging to their health. In-service and pre-service professional development work needs to be infused by the hard-nosed commercial question asked of business managers by Sutherland and Cooper (1990): 'How often do organisations protect, support and nurture this most valuable asset, the human resource?' The ethical and philosophical aspects of this question now cut little ice in a climate of market force economics, so it is worth noting that the authors posed it as a central *economic* question. How, then, can we reduce this wasteful loss of trained personnel from our schools?

Aims: To use an experiential approach to classroom management skills, together with trust-building exercises so that course members will:

- be willing to identify and disclose difficulties in classroom management skills, in a group of similarly willing colleagues;

- subject the 'self' to scrutiny in the knowledge that the teacher as a person is a key factor in the classroom equation;

- work on case material and examples with colleagues to generate a comprehensive repertoire of possible responses to challenging situations;

- practise these responses, first, in the relatively safe environment of the INSET DAY, by discussion, role play and simulation;
- have an opportunity to take the developing skills and attitudes into real classrooms, practise and evaluate them;
- become able to set up support networks with colleagues, thus continuing the enhancement of skills and confidence in a supportive environment.

Day one

9.00–10.30 Ice-breaking, setting the scene, creating a safe learning environment. Beginning to share one's 'self'. (The opening session is of great importance. All learning groups need to gel. The members send out messages to each other about safety, openness, support, comfort. The key tasks here are to help the group to relax, feel comfortable with each other and willing to 'risk' being honest and real. If this does not happen, we can waste a lot of time pretending that all is well, showing off about 'my' skills, spinning a complex web of counterproductive defensive strategies.)

Useful exercises for this can be found in Chapters 2 and 3:

'Ice-breaking' (p. 20): The 'Eyes' exercise, relaxation, humour, enhances trusts and social openness, forms working groups.

'Ice-breaking' (p. 21): 'Classroom nightmares' encourages disclosure, sense of collegiality and mutual support; gives 'permission' to admit difficulties.

Contexts, Definitions, Responsibility (p. 8): the case of Bryan and its complexity can be a useful focus of discussion. This can get too cerebral; group leader needs to chair in the direction of practical implications.

Agenda-setting (p. 21): Heraldic shield; this is a good disclosure exercise on values, self-perception and practice. Sensitive handling of the material shared is essential.

Bad/Good Teacher (p. 23): Raises awareness of the high significance of the inter- and intra-personal in effective teaching and classroom management.

10.30–11.00 Coffee. (Do not underestimate the positive potential of the social breaks!)

11.00–12.30 'Me!' (The key factor in the classroom equation is the teacher. There can be no abdication of this responsibility. This session is an opportunity to share, disclose values, begin to explore the human being who inhabits the teacher's professional persona.)

Useful exercises for this session can be found in Chapter 4:

Value-clarification exercise (1, values in general) (p. 34) can be used to establish and explore the reality of value variations in a small group. What are the implications of absence of consensual values in a working group?

Value-clarification exercise (2, pupil behaviour related) (p. 37) is a second look at values, focusing specifically on an ambiguous, disruptive incident. It invites a *value* response to the incident.

12.30–1.30 Lunch.

1.30–3.00 The nature of teaching and learning. (An invitation to learn is an invitation to become voluntarily incompetent for a while, to be uncomfortable and at risk. To accept such a daunting invitation the learner has got to feel safe with the teacher.)

Useful exercises for this session can be found in Chapter 5.

My self-image (p. 47). This exercise builds on the bad/good teacher exercise suggested for the first of the morning sessions, to clarify the perception the teacher has of her/himself. It uses theory drawn from the psychology of the self to move towards enhancing professional self-esteem.

The Ideal Teacher (p. 47) asks what values are projected in my school about competence as a teacher. Are they consonant with my vision of myself as a teacher? Is there a rhetoric–reality gap in my school or classroom between what is declared and what is delivered?

Feeling Good as a Teacher (p. 48) is a partnered exercise to look at positive views of self and the avoidance of stress.

It is important to draw out of this session the idea that both teachers and pupils need to have self-esteem in the classroom if teaching is not to degenerate into a sterile battle to maintain 'my' self-esteem at the expense of 'yours'.

3.00–4.00 Constructing a personal action plan. By this point in the day, the group will have generated a range of issues that infuse work to be done enhancing classroom management skills, e.g.:

Contexts	Labelling theory, social realities, home background of pupils, teacher values, school values, pupil values, home values, governor values, government requirements, LEA, etc.
Curriculum	Response to National Curriculum, attempts to 'match' in a realistic way.
Power/leadership	Awareness of styles of leadership growing; task leaders/and social leaders.
Quality of relating	Am I genetically locked into my current styles of relating, or can I be dynamic and change where I feel I need to?
Skills	What is good pedagogy? What new skills do I need? (Non-verbal skills, group dynamics?)
Rewards/sanctions	Do I run a reward-rich classroom? Do I compliment? How do I see my attitude to sanctions? Is it knee-jerk, or well thought out?

Self-esteem exercise (for everyone in the school)

Run the course today through some of the conceptual filters mentioned above. Is the course a safe place to work? Who helped to make it so? How?

Given the experience of the day, you may now feel able to identify an initial action plan. Such plans are always specific to individual schools or teachers, but it may help to discuss your plan with a colleague. Figure 8.1 may help to structure your planning (cf. Gelatt, 1962).

(1) PROBLEM ⟶ (2) RELEVANT ⟶ (3) GAP ⟶ (4) POSSIBILITIES
TO BE   DATA   FILLING
TACKLED   ASSEMBLY   (5) DESIRABILITIES

                                                     (6) DECISION;
Figure 8.1 An initial action plan.   ACTION

Each step contains within it a number of sub-tasks:

(1) *Problem identification*: What aspects of my professional performance diminish its effectiveness? What 'bits' of me reduce my ability to relate? Which values block clear thinking on classroom management issues?
    Problem analysis: How can I see this issue in manageable chunks? How can I clarify it?

(2) *Data assembly*: What do I need to know to respond to the issue I have identified? Where can I find out? Macro-influence (NCC, SEAC, Education Reform Act, etc.), and micro-influences (colleague, parents, pupils who are saboteurs, helpers, sustainers, facilitators, etc.).

(3) *Gap filling*: Constant monitoring for new and pertinent data, willingness to re-evaluate old data stock.

(4) *Problem-solving*: Given the issue, the database, what are the *possible* ways of responding? (This is about logic, feasibility and cool, clear thinking.)

(5) *Desirability*: Introduces the question of *values*. Given the generation of 'n' possible courses of action, what decision will be produce an operable consensus? Who else (if anyone) would it help to talk to?

(6) *Action*: Given these possibilities, I see course 'z' as an operable and desirable action. Who will help me in this? Who will hinder me? What specifically can I do to enhance the helper influence? How can I reduce the hindering influence?

To end the first day's work (or to conclude any session) a summarizing 'round' offers a final opportunity to everyone to share insights, get a feel for the rest of the group's perception of the day or simply discharge feelings that have not come out earlier. It is important that each comment is simply accepted, with no response, repartee, etc. from the floor.

Each group member is asked to complete a phrase in turn. The following are examples (choose one):

'One important thing I will take away from today is . . .'

'One surprise I got today was . . .'

'An important insight into my own teaching today was . . .'

'One thing I have appreciated about today is . . .'

If the group leader senses some discontent or lack of ease in the group, it can be very helpful to couple the 'appreciate' round with a prior 'resent' round. 'One thing I have resented about today is . . .'. This gets things to the surface and on to an open agenda. It also gives the group a clear message that it really is OK to be open. The material is simply received, not responded to.

Although this may seem some distance from pupil behaviour, the day can teach volumes about learning climates if the material is well used. The second day focuses more specifically on 'problems'.

Day two
9.00–10.30 Crisis. The case material at the beginning of Chapter 6, 'A Violent Incident' (p. 51), can be used to elicit a wide range of possible pre-emptive and reactive strategies. The suggestions can be role-played or simply discussed. If it is decided to discuss rather than role-play, it helps to keep the discussion focused on *behaviour*, operationalizing all suggestions as far as possible. There is a big temptation for participants to be too general, e.g. 'I would tell him to sit down.' Press for behavioural statements such as, 'I would say, "Would you sit down, please, Tom", or "Get your backside on to that chair, lad."'

10.30–11.00 Coffee.

11.00–12.30 Crisis 2. Draw from the group (e.g. by using the material drawn from the classroom nightmares exercise in Chapter 3), an example of an issue from their experience which is particularly challenging. In threes, ask them to

    (a) identify the factors that are at play in the incident (cf. Figure 2.1);

    (b) share as a whole group the full range of factors identified;

    (c) work in threes on *specific* behaviours that would respond to each of the factors;

    (d) discuss results as a whole group.

12.30–1.30 Lunch

1.30–3.00 The significance of the group. Use the exercise in Chapter 6 (p. 60) to raise awareness of what happens in a group. In particular, draw out the importance of the balance between *dominant* and *affiliative* non-verbal communication. Refer back to the case material of the previous exercise to re-examine it in the light of group dynamics. Practise non-verbal communicating (Chapter 6), and invite colleagues to do an analysed presentation as described at the end of the same chapter.

3.00–4.00 Loose ends. It is important to leave time for course members to raise any final issues – frequently to do with the rare but anxiety-provoking 'heavy incident'. Do not duck the discussion, and use Chapter 5 for exemplar material. There are no magic potions or panaceas – simply professional graft and problem-solving strategies. Have a final round of completions of the phrase, 'One thing I have appreciated about this course is ...' (you need to be comfortable with the '... nothing' contribution!) and/or, 'My next course of action on this issue will be to ...'.

All of the above relies on a warm, facilitative and knowledgeable group leader. It is a skill-raising and attitude-examining course, not a lecture course in social psychology.

Finally, course members can be invited to take back to their school the following checklist on 'Elton issues'. It places their learning in a whole-school context, and challenges the organization to action. The most difficult challenge to the teacher is not to *control* the pupils in the classroom; it is to establish a climate in which learning can take place.

THE ELTON RECOMMENDATIONS – SCHOOL AUDIT

What special attention is given to new teachers and the process of induction? (R7)

What is the quality of communication – within school (teachers, pupils), with parents, governors, the community and outside agencies? (R15)

How would you describe the sense of community within the school, its ethos and its relationship with its host community? (R16, R17)

Is there a visible, operating system of managerial support (referral procedures, back-up, case conferences) and of peer support (safe, respecting groups)? (R19)

Are decisions on pupil behaviour monitored for their effect on teacher and pupil morale? (R20)

Are such decisions clear, consistent, based on principle, with a declared, healthy balance between punishment and reward? (R23)

Are they also characterized by fairness, consistency and flexibility, with a clear distinction between major and minor infractions? (R23, R24, R25)

Can you be sure that no group punishment or humiliating punishments occur? (R26, R27)

Is a serious effort made to detect at the earliest opportunity any bullying or racial harassment? (R28)

Are victims supported and protected in the long term? Does the school have an ethos where such attacks are reported by pupils easily? (R28, R29)

Are the behavioural implications of curricular decisions fully monitored (material, teaching methods, pupil grouping)? (R30, R32)

Is the potential of PSE and the pastoral care system maximized in developing positive pupil behaviour? (R36, R37)

Is there a *systematic* collection of pupil views on school behaviour, and is use made of those views? (R39)

What trained counsellor presence do you have on the staff? (R43)

Is there a clear 'care of premises' policy which ensures a clean and attractive working environment for all? (R44)

Is the school regularly decorated with the work of students, as a way of enhancing pride in the common facilities? (R46)

In constructing the timetable is due attention given to the behavioural implications of times, movement and class–teacher match? (R51)

Are senior staff regularly visible at strategic points during the mass circulation of pupils? (R52)

Is there a clear, planned policy on behaviour over the lunch break, with training for non-teaching staff involved? (R54, R55, R56)

Are pupils involved by the use of records of achievement, compacts, or other means in taking more responsibility for themselves and their progress? (R75)

Do pupil records include information about their pastoral needs as well as their academic needs? (R80)

Has the school explored the potential benefits of 'support teams' as an alternative to premature exclusion? (R86)

Does the school have a declared, monitored policy on the issues of gender and cultural difference? Are staff trained in the skills needed to respond appropriately (e.g. in responding effectively to non-verbal or verbal behaviour which comes from pupils of different cultural backgrounds to their own)? (R89–R93)

Does the school have a clear policy and practice on truancy? Has liaison and consultation taken place with EWOs, police and other involved agencies? Are random checks carried out by senior staff on individual lessons? Are the governors fully involved in policy-making and informed regularly on outcomes in practice? (R99–R100, R101, R108)

Teachers know how complex a skill classroom management is. They know, too, that there is no 'pack' that can solve the problem – if only there were! Packs can help, but in the final analysis it is about *management*, problem definition, decision-making, value clarification, self-audit, skill development and ability to operate beyond the manual.

I have two final points to make, one about schools, the other about teachers.

Most children in schools are sane, well-behaved, normally challenging youngsters, engaged in the difficult task of becoming adults. It is actually fun to work with them and deeply satisfying. They must constitute about 80 per cent of our pupils. A further 15 per cent, in addition to growing up, have to face a vast range of disadvantages: unsupportive homes, poverty, parental criminality, sudden bereavement, physical or sexual abuse and that vast range of unwarranted things that can burden a child in today's world. We need to, and do, respond to these damaged children, but central to my argument has been the position that to set up behavioural management strategies geared to the needs of a few children and to apply them to all children is indefensible. The most damaged 5 per cent require even more specialized response. In strategic terms, Figure 8.2 outlines the broader shape of response. Each column can include elements from the other columns; the figure is used to illustrate possible foci for each sector of school pupils.

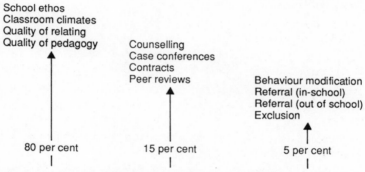

Figure 8.2 Typical response foci for different sectors of the school population.

And, finally, for teachers. Elton speaks of how they have 'a traditional reluctance to talk about discipline problems or to let colleagues into their classrooms'. He argues that this 'feeds into a spiral of less effective group management and mounting stress'. The Report goes on to make one of its most helpful suggestions.

> Support from collegues as professional equals, which we call peer support, is a way of breaking out of that spiral. The peer support group is a valuable resource, which is as yet little used in British schools.... A peer support group is led by a 'facilitator', who is responsible for convening the group and chairing its discussions. It meets regularly on a voluntary basis to talk about management skills. ... Its discussions are a very effective form of in-service training ... it helps to break down the tradition of isolation by opening the classroom door ... it helps to reduce occupational stress.

And with that, the end of our journey. No package, no definitive procedures, no infallible recipes. What more fitting closure to an exploratory text like this than T. S. Eliot's words:

> And the end of all our exploring
> Will be to arrive where we started
> And know the place for the first time.
>
> ('Little Gidding', V, in *Four Quartets*)

Appendix
Case material with commentary

The following case material is offered on the grounds that it can be helpful to cast an objective eye over someone else's problem. All of this material has been shared by classroom teachers on professional development courses. Confidentiality has been protected by changing names and other non-significant detail.

BUSINESS STUDIES: THE PHANTOM SKIRT-LIFTER

The incident described below took place in a fourth-year class, doing business studies. The teacher was experienced, but this was her first contact with the class in question.

Each pupil had been allocated a work-station and PC by alphabetical order. The pupils seemed to be industrious and to be enjoying the lessons.

At our third meeting, I was helping a pupil to use a word-processing program, standing between two work-stations, and leaning across to use the keyboard. I had my back to two pupils further down the row, and was engrossed in the teaching task. I suddenly became aware that my skirt had been lifted up when I felt the touch of a hand on my leg. I turned round quickly to see all the pupils behind me giggling, but without being able to determine who the culprit had been. I remonstrated with the two girls closest to me ('Don't be so childish'), but did not know them sufficiently well to pursue it further. One girl looked guilty, but I decided to leave it till later, and turned back to helping the pupil with whom I had initially been working.

To my astonishment and fury, I felt my skirt being lifted again. I whipped round as quickly as I could, reaching out to grab the hand of the culprit. Unfortunately, she was quicker than I, and I only managed to crack my hand against a printer, and cut myself quite badly.

I told both of the girls whom I suspected to wait outside, instructed the class to continue working, and went to have my finger dressed.

This incident seems to raise issues of:

non-verbal behaviour (peripheral vision of the whole class, when working with individuals);

verbal response to misbehaviour, whose originator is unknown (when and how do I investigate?);

social learning for pupils about privacy and personal integrity (when is a joke an invasion of personal space?);

unanticipated escalation of an incident (the nosebleed, the epileptic fit, physical aggression).

It can be used for discussion, role play of possible responses, values exploration and analysis of whole-school issues, e.g. leaving a class, referral of incidents to year heads, and so on.

ENGLISH: THE WILD BUNCH

This is an account by an excellent young teacher, working in a difficult inner-city area, of a very demanding teaching challenge.

I had been warned that the fifth-year group I was to take for English had been difficult throughout their school career. I was astounded that so many demanding pupils could be put into one class.

John and Paul play up to each other, and are well able to reduce the whole class to laughter. They both have loud voices, can be genuinely funny, but John is unpredictable and Paul can be supersensitive. Both can be verbally gross (swearing), and rude. I could plan a strategy for the two of them, but the other 27 present quite a challenge too.

Belinda and Debbie tend to be silly and giggly, apparently needing attention. I can 'control' them, in that both can be cowed by a loud voice or threat of report to the year head. I know that Belinda's mother died of cancer last year, and that Debbie is fostered, and that I ought to do something more than control them by yelling. But can I find the time? Geoff and Stevie are known as the 'gruesome twosome' in the staffroom, and they and Mickey and Stu invariably find each other like magnets. Individually they are OK – I can get reasonable work out of Geoff, if I give my Oscar-winning telling-off performance, but after a while even that begins to lose force. Mickey seems quiet, but he never does any work. He just stares into my eyes, with an expression just short of insolence.

Dawn and Suzanne 'hate school', and *try* to get minus house points. Dawn is lazy and resents being asked to work. I suspect she finds the work difficult, so I have tried to build up her self-esteem. She seems to spurn all attempts to be nice to her, feeling more comfortable with open warfare. My teaching material is deliberately geared to respond to the full ability range – these two have me at a loss.

Barbara, Janet, Mandy and Susie are not nastily disruptive, just silly and giggly. They are quite intelligent, but seem to have no concentration. Mandy started off quite well, but my attempts to keep her on track have left her disliking me intensely. Barbara is a bit of a moaner.

Roy and Daniel have very concerned parents and respond to my threat to contact them. They are a strain for me, since they do seem to want to do some work, but I am up to my ears in coping with 'the wild bunch'! I am really teaching for all I'm worth, here, and seem to be getting nowhere. Help! What do you do when the whole lot seems to overwhelm you?

My feeling is that so many difficult children should be managed differently – smaller groups, split up in some way. The whole chemistry of the group is wrong, and my constant attempt to hold it together has spoilt my relationship with the well-behaved and hard-working minority.

My head of department tells me that my level of self-criticism is far higher than that of most young teachers. Am I expecting too much? Behaviourally, I look for self-discipline, and academically, application to the best of one's ability. I never thought I would say this, but I suspect that the ability-based grouping has pulled this group into a downward spiral of lowered expectations. Would they fare better in a mixed-ability group?

I have included this case because it, or something like it, is presented at almost every course I run on pupil behaviour. The complexity of the challenge is obvious: home influence, issues of curricular matching, balancing social and academic learning, being realistic without being under-demanding. This is the teaching reality that too frequently the layperson is ignorant of.

Could a situation like this be happening in your school? If not, what strategies are used to avoid it, or respond to it if it begins to occur? Are there contextual issues here, about general levels of behaviour accepted from children in the school? How effective is the support and referral system? Do the pupils have an awareness of the whole-school support their teacher has?

This study is useful for looking at the preventive and whole-school dimensions of responses to pupils' behaviour.

A SUPERVISION PERIOD WITH A DIFFICULT CLASS

One of the science department was ill, so I was asked to supervise the work of a group of fourth-years for a double period. I hate supervisions (I should be preparing or marking my own classes' work), because it is much more difficult to control classes one rarely sees. I had taught some of them the previous year, so I was prepared for trouble.

I arranged to take the class in my own room, so I was meeting them on my own ground instead of in a science lab. I asked the science technician to send them, their books and their textbooks to my room. They arrived noisily (the disruptive effect of an absent teacher), and I lined them up outside the room. When they had settled down, I let them into the room.

One boy, whose name I did not know, attempted to move furniture. I made him put the desk and chair where they had been, and sat him down. A second boy was hiding round a corner. I moved him straight to the front of the class, where he was no further trouble.

The class followed lunch, and one person, whom I could not identify, started making vomiting noises. At first I thought someone was ill, but then identified the grinning clown, and put him next to my desk to work. The cure was instantaneous! Another pupil seemed not to have got down to work – I fixed him with a stare, stood up and wandered to the back of the class, where I could see him, but he could not see me without turning round. A couple of boys on the right started to talk in whispers – I said, in a quiet voice, 'Get on with the work you are supposed to be doing', and they did. Calm reigned, I was in control.

I returned to the teacher's desk, at the front of the class, to begin my own work, and had just started when someone in the room began to whistle quietly. I pretended not to notice and continued to do my own work. The whistling got louder, so I suggested that the whistler should save his talent to delight the music teacher. There were a few sniggers, almost an easing of tension, and all of us got back to work.

When the bell rang for the end of the first period, there was some general chatter, which I quickly quelled. 'This is a double period. You, and I, have plenty of work to do, so get on with it.' The session seemed to be going relatively smoothly. I was feeling quite pleased with myself, when in the industrious silence, someone let out a long, loud, anti-social noise. (He farted.) The class roared with delight.

I had no idea who the guilty party was, waffled on about the social inappropriateness of it, deeply conscious that such behaviour was commonplace in clubs and pubs up and down the land. I felt strangely depressed. The lesson ended, and I returned to tell colleagues in the staffroom. They laughed, too.

Some issues for possible discussion here are the management of 'cover', working with pupils one does not know well (domination/affiliation as in Chapter 5), and value variation (the colleagues' reaction). The teacher seems to have carried off some challenging tasks very competently. The depression she mentions at the end draws attention to strong peer support. We need to look after each other.

MATHEMATICS: THE SPITTING OLYMPICS

This incident involves a second-year group of 26 pupils. The class had been working quietly on percentages, coming to my desk to have work checked or to be helped with difficulties. I check carefully that I see everyone's work, and that my view of the class is not obscured.

Halfway through the lesson, Gregory came out to my desk and said someone had spit on his jacket, which was hanging on the back of his chair. I had not seen anything and, like Greg, did not know who had done it. I told all the children to sit down, at which point Robbie said, 'Ergh! Miss! There is spit all over my desk.' Robbie sits behind Greg. I asked, 'OK, I want to know who did this.' No one answered. Complete silence.

Teacher: 'You may be used to living in filth, but I am not. Who knows anything about this filthy trick?' Silence.

Teacher: 'Well that makes some people in this room liars, because someone knows something.' Still no response. 'Right. When the bell goes, we will all stay here until I find the culprit. Get on with your work.'

The lesson ended and I told everyone to remain seated. 'OK,' I said, pointing to the row next to the window, 'you would have to be in the spitting olympics to reach over here. You can go. And you four, on the front, would have to be contortionists to do it from there, so you can go, too.' I was beginning to feel anxious. I had seven left in the room – what if someone was willing to brazen it out? 'Well,' I said, 'I hope that there is still some consideration in the person who did it. I want you to own up, now.'

'It was me,' said Caroline.

'Why on earth did you do a filthy and stupid thing like that, girl?' I asked.

'Don't know, Miss.'

'Well, that just shows your mentality, doesn't it? You can write me 200 words on "spitting", and I'm putting you on detention. Get out!'

Course tutors may wish to explore with teachers the initial thoughtfulness of the teacher and her classroom organization, her response to crisis, detective work and eventual dealing with the pupil. There seem to be some issues here on culture clash. How might the ending be varied?

TYPING AT A TERTIARY COLLEGE: EPILEPSY AND RAPE

Not all pupil misbehaviour comes from an intention to disrupt. Sometimes a young person is distraught because of something that has happened outside the school. It is still the teacher who has to respond.

Joan was eighteen when she came on a YTS course for out-of-work school-leavers. I had been told by the Careers Office that she was an epileptic on medication and that she was adopted. During the course Joan was always seeking advice and confirmation of her actions. 'Should I do ...', 'Would you do ...'. As far as typing was concerned, even when the instructions for a task were written down – e.g. type on A4 in double line spacing – she would say, 'Miss, would you type this on A4 in double line spacing?'

Joan spoke of her parents and brothers, about how good they were, how much money she had, what clothes she had, etc. She also spoke of her grandmother. One Friday afternoon about 3.30 while the class were doing a typing exam Joan started to shout in the class, 'I've been raped. I don't care if anyone knows it. Nobody wants me. Nobody loves me. Me mam and dad don't want me now I've been raped ...' I was filling in the returns (Joan was sitting in her usual place about three feet from me). I went to her and put my arm round her (she now had tears in her eyes). I whispered in her ear, 'Now then Joan, what's the matter? If it's the typing that's upsetting you, leave it till Monday, it's not worth getting upset about.'

She shouted, flinging her arms about, 'I've been raped – I don't care who knows it!' Arm still round her I said quietly, 'Joan, don't say today what you might regret on Monday.'

All the while Barbara was saying, 'What did Joan say?' (Barbara was well known for her 'elephant ears'.)

Luckily the rest of the class weren't as interested and as it was now about five to four I asked them to start packing up while I was still with Joan.

Joan was about 5'10" and had teamed up with a tiny girl, Jo, of 4'10". Her friend came over and asked if Joan was going for the bus. I said I would take her home to Esh or phone for her mother, but she wanted to go with Jo, who promised to see her on the bus to Esh.

I was concerned that

(a) she was an epileptic and could have a fit or take an overdose of her tablets, which she always carried.

(b) if she had been 'put out' by her mam and dad, and she said her grandmother didn't want her now she'd been raped – who would she go to? She only knew Jo, who was equally immature (yet had turned up trumps by quietly trying to talk sense into her when she was ranting and raving).

What should I do?

I went to my head of department as by now (4.20ish) no one else was in the department. He listened and then asked what I thought should be done. I suggested he rang Joan's mother. He rang the number and handed me the phone. Help, what do I say?

The final piece of case material offered in this supplement concerns something that happened in a primary school. As with the case of Joan, Helen's behaviour in school is being affected by things going on outside the school. It would be a mistake (certainly not one that teachers make) for parents, governors and our political masters to think that schools function in some kind of moral vacuum. We are not responsible for the deprivation, cruelty, sheer bad example and negative attitudes that our children experience outside school, and then bring into the school with them – we are not responsible, but we have to respond.

In this final study, Helen can be assigned an age which matches the teaching phase of the course participants. Sadly, the experience is one suffered by pupils across the full range of our schools. Sometimes the behaviour of the children in school is disruptive; at other times, and more insidiously, the behavioural disturbance is turned inwards.

HELEN E: A CASE STUDY IN FOUR PARTS

1. Helen E is eight years old and has just joined your class after moving into the neighbourhood from a school 150 miles away. You have had no personal meeting with the parents, but have spoken briefly with the mother, who phoned to inform the school that Helen would arrive for the new academic year. Helen arrives in new blazer, clean white blouse and socks, evidently new shoes. Her hair is long, brushed to a gleam. She is shy, not speaking at all to the other children – only replying when directly questioned. You notice that she *never* smiles. During the first morning you have placed her in a group working together on a 'Summer Holidays' frieze. The children in the group are socially adept, chatter busily and happily. Helen has not spoken. On two occasions she has nodded. You move closer to observe more carefully. Jenny, in your hearing, asks Helen to come to her party. 'I'm not allowed', is the reply. 'Why not?' is the chorused response as the other three girls stop work in amazement. 'Because our religion believes that parties are vanities,' Helen stumbles on. 'What-ities?' giggles Lindsay. You set in to rescue Helen, puzzled and feeling slightly ill at ease.

Please discuss the following:

  (a) Your reaction in general to the above. How does it make you feel?
  (b) What further information would you like to get? How would you set about getting it? What difficulties do you foresee?
  (c) Who would you like to involve in your plans in responding to Helen? How?
  (d) What specific decisions would you take now? Action (if any)?

For course tutors
The purpose of this exercise is to avoid teachers de-skilling themselves. A 'referral technician' approach underuses the experience and skill of teachers. The discussion should be used to draw to the surface a number of issues, as follows:

– Our response to pedagogical challenge is value influenced. 'Who am I in this encounter?' is a prior question to 'What should I do?' Help the group to articulate anxieties, strongly influential values and attitudes – without undermining them. Perhaps a model of decision-making may help (see Figure A.1).

– Lack of information can leave us thrashing around in the dark. Records from other school? (cf. Maria Colwell death: recommendations on communications within and between schools). Is the phone enough? Record cards? Access? 'Children at Risk' file? Meet parents?

– Feeling alone with difficult decisions is paralysing. What support networks exist for teachers in my school who face difficult problems? Case conference? (size?) Involve outside agencies? (when?) Interminable data collection not enough – action?

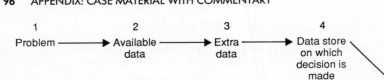

Figure A.1 Decision-making model.

– Is there a clear system of in-school communication and extra-school referral/advice?

I don't think there are infallible procedures that have cross-school validity, but here I would want contact with the previous school (head and class teacher, phone) a copy of the record card, a meeting with the parents and – most important – to make Helen feel part of the class and special, like all the other children. This is the start.

2. Six weeks have passed, Helen has established herself as a serious, rarely smiling member of a small group of extrovert, accepting girls. Jenny, Lindsay and Nicola are protective of and helpful to Helen, whose work is painstaking but slow. The three girls regularly go swimming, with their parents taking turns to act as chauffeur/supervisor. Helen has often been asked to go swimming, and to two parties. She is clearly upset at her inability to join her friends, but stoutly declares she may not because of religious conviction. To your surprise, she agrees one day to go shopping with the three girls on the way home from school. You see it as a breakthrough – and make encouraging (and cautionary/watch the road) comments to them. Next day Helen is not at school. She returns after two days' absence with a note saying she had hurt herself in a fall. She is deeply introverted, working silently and without even eye contact with the three girls. She is visibly in pain from the fall and moves very awkwardly in PE. You chat gently to her and hear the strange (in the mouth of a child) phrase: 'Me dad chastised me for not going straight home. ' 'Is that why you can't jump?' you ask gently. 'No,' she says, 'that's because I fell down at home.'

Please discuss the following:

(a) Your reaction. What does this make you feel? Is it easy/comfortable coping with such feelings? What would help you at the emotional level?

(b) Who else would you now want involved? How would you set about doing this?

(c) What decisions would you take? Actions?

(d) What do you think Helen needs from you?

For course tutors

– Although we try not to get emotionally involved with pupils, that does not mean we don't respond emotionally. Burying feelings can be a great psychological strain, and can distort our perception of what is going on. Students working with me have expressed feelings of anger, contempt, shock, impotence, fear or sadness when confronting such case material. Simply to articulate and share such feelings with colleagues can give great help. This is not a therapy session – it is pursuing the question, 'Who am I in this encounter?'

– Initial suspicions of physical or sexual abuse leave us ambivalent – wanting to make sure our children are safe, but not wanting to make unjust or foolish invasions of parental privacy. It should always be safe for teachers to articulate such anxiety in confidence to a head or case conference. Draw out from the group what procedures they use. Discuss the use (support, depth) of case conferences – and their problems (time, confidentiality).

– Action must involve checking that physical abuse is not taking place. More data. What liaison with outside support agencies exists (NSPCC, police, social services)? Personal contacts are very useful.

– If Helen is being physically abused, then she is suffering what Kempe and Kempe (1978) call a 'developmental insult'; that is, instead of having an environment conducive to emotional growth, she is being stunted. Our job is to offer in the classroom that safe, respecting, supportive, praising environment which is appropriate. Sometimes we withdraw in fear from abused children, compounding their pain. As teachers we are sometimes the only source of respect and affection some children have. Discuss precisely the things you would do to help Helen respond to the challenge she faces.

3. Christmas is approaching and the excitement of its preparation grips the children. The Nativity play is being prepared. Helen, who you speculate has mentioned this at home, brings a note to school: 'Dear Mrs ———, We would like it to be known that Helen is not to take part in the parties, plays and games related to Christmas. This is on account of our religious beliefs. She can read on her own.' Helen gives you the note, in tears, because she has been working on a Bethlehem tableau with her friends. She had told her mother, and had been punished by her father. 'How do you mean, punished, Helen?' you ask. 'He chastises me,' she declares, earnestly, biblically. 'I don't know what that means, love,' you say. 'He hits me with a belt.'

Please discuss (reflecting your practice as far as possible):

(a) your reactions;

(b) any further data you would want and how you would get it;

(c) decisions/actions you would want to take;

(d) how you would respond to Helen.

For course tutors

Two themes will be emerging:

(a) The attempt to stop the beating. We need help for this from outside agencies and their involvement needs to be planned in advance with clear procedural steps;

(b) The classroom response to Helen – how do we best combat the development damage she is facing? This group will have great experience and talent here. We need to liberate it and get them talking about it.

4. In mid-February Helen complains of a 'sore' tummy, is very pale, and suddenly vomits in class. In helping her out of the room, it is obvious that she finds it painful to be touched. Appendicitis floats into your mind. The pain is such that she is crying, and having tried unsuccessfully to call the parents you take her to the casualty department of the local hospital. Your head covers your responsibility at school. The doctors shows you a large, fist-shaped bruise, clearly showing four knuckle marks into the floating ribs and lower abdomen.

Please discuss your next steps. (Helen's father is successfully prosecuted and receives a prison sentence. Helen stays at home with her mother and continues to attend your school.)

For course tutors

Issues here are: careful documentation of all proceedings, clear liaison with all outside agencies, individualized curriculum planning for Helen which includes meticulous consideration of her social and emotional needs.

Estimates of *sexual* abuse of children suggest that between 10 and 20 per cent of all children suffer in this way at some point in their life.

Physical abuse is certainly more common, but there is overlap. Sadly, the problem is one that most teachers have to face.

Each small group will be asked to produce an 'Action manual' on a flip-chart.

1. Observation skills (what 'good practice' exists in this group); records; identification;

2. Response skills (scrutinizing our pedagogy);

3. Management skills – organizing, documenting, liaising, supporting in order to 'manage' the learning and response to a 'special child'.

Bibliography

Apter, S. J. (1982) *Troubled Children, Troubled Systems*. Oxford: Pergamon.

Argyle, M. (1983) *The Psychology of Interpersonal Behaviour*. Harmondsworth: Penguin.

Argyle, M. (1988) *Bodily Communication*. 2nd edn. London: Methuen.

Aronson, E. and Mettee, D. R. (1965) Dishonest behaviour as a function of differential levels of induced self-esteem. *Journal of Personality and Social Psychology*, 9: 121–7.

Axelrod, S. (1977) *Behaviour Modification for the Classroom Teacher*. New York: McGraw-Hill.

Best, R., Jarvis, C. and Ribbins, P. (eds) (1980) *Perspectives on Pastoral Care*. London: Heinemann.

Bird, C. *et al.* (1980) *Disaffected Pupils*. A Report to the Department of Education and Science by the Education Studies Unit, Brunel University.

Blocher, D. H. (1974) *Developmental Counselling*. New York: Ronald Press.

Blomberg, A. and Golembiewski, R. T. (1976) *Learning and Change in Groups*. Harmondsworth: Penguin.

Borba, M. C. and Borba, C. (1978) *Self-Esteem: A Classroom Affair*. San Francisco: Harper & Row.

Brammer, L. M. and Shostrum, E. L. (1982) *Therapeutic Psychology*. 4th edn. Englewood Cliffs, NJ: Prentice-Hall.

Burns, R. B. (1979) *The Self Concept: Theory, Measurement, Development and Behaviour*. London: Longman.

Burns, R. B. (1982) *Self Concept Development and Education*. London: Holt, Rinehart & Winston.

Caldwell, B. and Miskow, J. (1984) School-based budgeting: a financial strategy for meeting the needs of students. *Educational Administration*, Review 2.1. Cited in H. L. Gray (ed.) (1988) *Management Consultancy in Schools*. London: Cassell.

Cantor, S. (1984) *The Schizophrenic Child*. Milton Keynes: Open University Press.

Carkhuff, R. R. and Berenson, B. G. (1977) *Beyond Counselling and Therapy*. 2nd edn. New York: Holt, Rinehart & Winston.

Cartwright, D. and Zanders, A. (eds) (1968) *Group Dynamics: Research and Theory*. London: Tavistock.

Catholic Herald (1978) Corporal punishment. 8 December.

Cleugh, M. F. (1971) *Discipline and Morale in School and College: A Study of Group Feeling*. London: Tavistock.

Cooper, C. L. (1981) *The Stress Check*. Englewood Cliffs, NJ: Prentice-Hall.

Coopersmith, S. (1967) *The Antecedents of Self-Esteem*. San Francisco: Freeman.

Department of Education and Science (DES) (1987) *Good Behaviour and Discipline in Schools*. London: HMSO.

DES (1989) *Report of the Committee of Inquiry into Discipline in Schools* (the Elton Report). London: HMSO.

Department of Health and Social Security (1988) *Working Together for the Protection of Children from Abuse*, Circular 4/88. London: DHSS.

Dunham, J. (1984) *Stress in Teaching*. London: Croom Helm.

Eaton, M. J. (1979) A study of some factors associated with early identification of persistent absenteeism. *Education Review*, **31**(3), 2–33.

Egan, G. (1982) *The Skilled Helper: Models, Skills and Methods for Effective Helping*. 2nd edn. Monterey, CA: Brookes/Cole.

Egan, G. (1986) *The Skilled Helper: A Systematic Approach to Effective Helping*. Monterey, CA: Brookes/Cole.

Eliot, T. S. (1959) Little Gidding, from *Four Quartets*. London: Faber & Faber.

Elliot-Kemp, J. (1992) *Managing Change and Development in Schools: A Practical Handbook*. Harlow: Longman.

Erikson, E. (1965) *Childhood and Society*. Harmondsworth: Penguin.

Everard, B. (1984) *Management in Comprehensive Schools: What Can Be Learned from Industry*. Centre for the Study of Comprehensive Schools, University of York.

Francis, P. (1975) *Beyond Control*. London: Allen & Unwin.

Galloway, D., Ball, T., Bloomfield, D. and Seyd, R. (1982) *Schools and Disruptive Pupils*. London: Longman.

Gelatt, H. B. (1962) Decision-making: a conceptual frame of reference for counselling. *Journal of Counselling Psychology*, **9**(3), 240–5.

Gilliland, J. and McGuiness, J. (1989) In N. Jones (ed.) *Special Educational Needs Review*, Vol. 2, *Special Educational Needs and Counselling*. London: Falmer Press.

Graham, D. (1972) *Moral Learning and Development*. London: Batsford.

Grunsell, R. (1980) *Beyond Control? Schools and Supervision*. London: Writers and Readers.

Handy, C. (1985) *Understanding Organisations*. 3rd edn. Harmondsworth: Penguin.

Hargreaves, D. (1976) *Deviance in the Classroom*. London: Routledge & Kegan Paul.

Heath, D. H. (1977) *Maturity and Competence*. New York: Gardner.

Heisler, V. (1961) Towards a process model of psychological health. *Journal of Counselling Psychology*, 11(1), 59–62.

Heller, Z. and Judd, J. (1991) Cracks appear at the chalkface. *Independent on Sunday*, 24 March.

Her Majesty's Inspectorate (HMI) (1987) *Good Behaviour and Discipline in Schools*. London: HMSO.

Inner London Education Authority (ILEA) (1986) *Suspensions and Expulsions from School, 1986–7*. London: ILEA.

ILEA (1988) Internal report cited in G. Smith (1989) Recent research on disruption in schools: a summary paper. Unpublished paper prepared for HMI, Course A319.

International Labour Organisation (ILO) (1981) Report in *The Guardian*, 4 July.

Jahoda, M. (1979) The impact of unemployment in the 1930s and the 1970s. *Bulletin of the British Psychological Society*, **32**, 309–14.

Jahoda, M. (1981) Work, employment and unemployment: values, theories and approaches in social research. *American Psychologist*, **36**, 184–91.

Jones, N. T. (1975) Emotionally disturbed children in ordinary schools. *British Journal of Guidance and Counselling*, July, 146.

Kempe, R. S. and Kempe, C. H. (1978) *Child Abuse: The Developing Child*. London: Open Books/Fontana.

Krumboltz, J. D. and Thoresen, C. E. (1976) *Counselling Methods*. New York: Holt, Rinehart & Winston.

Kyriacou, C. (1986) *Effective Teaching in Schools*. Oxford: Blackwell.

Lawlor, S. (1990) *Teachers Mistaught*. London: Centre for Policy Studies.

Lennhoff, F. G. (1965) *Forty-four Children Thinking Aloud: Therapeutic Group Discussion with Boys aged 10–17 in a Residential Setting*. Shrewsbury: Shotton Hall Publications.

McGuiness, J. B. (1983) Secondary education for all? In F. J. Coffield and R. D. Goodings (eds) *Sacred Cows in Education: Essays in Reassessment*. Edinburgh: Edinburgh University Press.

McGuiness, J. B. (1988) In P. Lang (ed.) *Thinking About Personal and Social Education in the Primary School*, pp. 319–23. Oxford: Blackwell.

McGuiness, J. (1989) *A Whole-School Approach to Pastoral Care*. London: Kogan Page.

McGuiness, J. and Craggs, S. (1986) Disruption as a school-generated problem. In D. Tattum (ed.) *Management of Disruptive Pupil Behaviour in Schools*. Chichester: John Wiley.

Mortimore, P. *et al.* (1988) *School Matters: The Junior Years*, Wells: Open Books.

Nelson-Jones, R. (1982) *The Meaning and Practice of Counselling Psychology*. Eastbourne: Holt, Rinehart & Winston.

Piaget, J. and Inhelder, B. (1969) *The Psychology of the Child*. New York: Basic Books.

Power, M. J., Alderson, M. R. and Phillipson, C. M. (1967) Delinquent schools. *New Society*, 29 July, 542–3.

Reynolds, D. (1976) Do schools make a difference? *New Society*, 19 October, 233–5.

Reynolds, D. and Sullivan, M. (1987) *The Comprehensive Experiment*. London: Falmer Press.

Rogers, C. R. (1962) *On Becoming a Person: A Therapist's View of Psychotherapy*. London: Constable.

Rogers, C. R. (1965) *Client-Centred Therapy*. London: Constable.

Rogers, C. R. (1969) *Freedom to Learn: A View of What Education Might Become*. Columbus, OH: Merrill.

Rogers, C. R. (1983) *Freedom to Learn for the Eighties*. Columbus, OH: Merrill.

Rutter, M., Maughan, B., Mortimore, P. and Ouston, J. (1979) *Fifteen Thousand Hours: Secondary Schools and Their Effects on Children*. Shepton Mallet, Somerset: Open Books.

Salzberger-Wittenberg, I. (1983) *The Emotional Experience of Teaching and Learning*. London: Routledge & Kegan Paul.

Sayer, J. (1988) Identifying the issues. In H. C. Gray (ed.) *Management Consultancy in Schools*. London: Cassell.

Schostak, J. D. (1982) *Maladjusted Schooling: Deviance, Social Control and Individuality in Secondary Schooling*. London: Falmer Press.

Schrag, P. and Divoky, D. (1981) *The Myth of the Hyperactive Child*. Harmondsworth: Penguin.

Smith, G. (1989) Recent research on disruption in schools: a summary paper. Unpublished paper prepared for HMI, Course A319.

Snygg, A. W. and Combs, D. (1959) *Individual Behaviour*. New York: Harper & Row.

Spiel, O. (1962) *Discipline without Punishment*. London: Faber & Faber.

Sprinthall, N. A. (1981) A new model for research in the service of guidance counselling. *Personal and Guidance Journal*, **59**(8).

Steed, D., Lawrence, J. and Young, P. (1983) Beyond the naughty child. *Times Educational Supplement*, 28 October.

Summerfield Report (1968) *Psychologists in Education Services*. London: HMSO.

Sutherland, V. J. and Cooper, C. L. (1990) *Understanding Stress: A Psychological Perspective for Health Professionals*. London: Chapman & Hall.

Tattum, D. (1982) *Disruptive Pupils in Schools and Units*. Chichester: John Wiley.

Tattum, D. (ed.) (1986) *Management of Disruptive Pupil Behaviour in Schools*. Chichester: John Wiley.

Thompson, S. and Kahn, J. (1970) *The Group Process as a Helping Technique*. Oxford: Pergamon.

Trower, P. *et al.* (1978) *Social Skills and Mental Health*. London: Methuen.

Truax, C. B. and Carkhuff, R. R. (1976) *Towards Effective Counselling and Psychotherapy*. Chicago: Aldine.

Vaughan, M. (1983) Disruptive teachers? *Times Educational Supplement*, 28 October.

Watts, A. (1983) *Education, Unemployment and the Future of Work.* Milton Keynes: Open University Press.

Wheldall, K. (ed.) (1991) *Discipline in Schools: Psychological Perspectives on the Elton Report.* London: Routledge.

Woodcock, M. *Team Development.* Aldershot: Gower.

INDEXES

Name index

Subject index